SOPHOCLES

Oedipus the King

translated by
DON TAYLOR

with commentary and notes by
ANGIE VARAKIS

Bloomsbury Methuen Drama
An imprint of Bloomsbury Publishing Plc

B L O O M S B U R Y

NEW DELHI • LONDON • OXFORD • NEW YORK • SYDNEY

Bloomsbury Publishing India Pvt. Ltd
Second Floor, Building No.4
DDA Complex LSC, Pocket C – 6 & 7
Vasant Kunj, New Delhi 110070
www.bloomsbury.com

First published in India 2017
This translation of Oedipus the King first published in 1986 by Eyre Methuen Ltd in Sophocles: The Theban Plays (subsequently Sophocles Plays: One) This edition first published in the United Kingdom by Bloomsbury Methuen Drama 2008
Reissued with a new cover design 2009
Reprinted 2010, 2013 (twice), 2014, 2015

Bloomsbury Methuen Drama
An imprint of Bloomsbury Publishing Plc
Bloomsbury is a registered trade mark of Bloomsbury Publishing Plc
This edition published with permission fromBloomsbury Publishing Plc
50 Bedford Square, London WC1B 3DP

British Library Cataloguing-in-Publication Data
A catalogue record for this book is available from the British Library.
Library of Congress Cataloging-in-Publication Data
A catalog record for this book is available from the Library of Congress.

ISBN : 978 93 86250 69 8
10 9 8 7 6
For sale in the Indian subcontinent only

Typeset by SX Composing DTP, Rayleigh, Essex
Printed and bound in India by Gopsons Papers Pvt. Ltd. Sivakasi

Contents

Sophocles: *c.* 496–406 BC

Sophocles' long life and prolific career as a dramatist (over 120 plays) coincides with the unfolding of fifth-century Athenian democracy, that high classical period, which witnessed wars with both Persia and Sparta, Pericles' golden years of democratic rule, the building and decoration of the Parthenon, an unprecedented acceleration in philosophy, science and the arts. Sophocles outlived the younger playwright Euripides and met such figures as the dramatist Aeschylus, the politician Pericles, the philosopher Socrates, the historians Herodotus and Thucydides and many others. On a personal level, he is said to have married one Nicostrate and fathered a son, Iophon, with whom, allegedly, his relationship was bad. He also had a grandson who was named after him.

Our biographical information about Sophocles is related more to his life outside the theatre since most of his plays are lost, while the dates of his surviving seven dramas are uncertain – of the seven plays that survive entire we only have fixed dates for *Philoctetes* (409) and *Oedipus at Colonus* (401). However, most scholars agree that there are good stylistic reasons for placing *Ajax* and *Women of Trachis* in the early period of his career (late 440s and late 430s respectively) and *Electra* at a much later date (possibly about 415). *Oedipus the King* is most commonly placed in the early 420s while *Antigone* is more confidently positioned between 442 and 440 due to the claim that Sophocles was elected general around 440 after his success with his production of *Antigone*.

All of the tragedies mentioned in the chronology were produced at the City Dionysia festival, an annual event to honour the gods and display Athens' wealth and prosperity. Information regarding Sophocles' personal life relies mainly on various anecdotal sources which were compiled in later antiquity into a biography entitled *The Life of Sophocles*. This chronology has confined itself to those dates which are most trustworthy.

496/5 Sophocles, son of Sophillos, is born into a wealthy family of merchants at the *deme* (locality) of Colonus, near Athens. As a young boy he must have received the usual aristocratic education which involved training in music, dancing and athletics.

490 The first Persian invasion at Marathon is defeated by the Athenian navy. It is said that the tragedian Aeschylus participated in this battle.

480 The second Persian invasion is defeated by the Athenian navy at Salamis. Sophocles, already known for his talent in the performing arts, is invited to participate in the victory song celebrating the Athenian military success. The youngest of the three famous tragic poets, Euripides, is born.

468 Sophocles enters the drama competition at the City Dionysia festival (possibly with the play *Triptolemos*) and is awarded first prize, defeating the elder and already established tragedian Aeschylus. Sophocles' successful debut makes him instantly popular.

462 The political leaders Pericles and Ephialtes reform the Athenian constitution giving more power to the people against the aristocratic few. The golden age of democracy is about to begin. Sophocles may not have been in favour of such radical reforms against traditional values.

458 Aeschylus' trilogy *Oresteia* is presented, reflecting in a positive way the current political situation.

449 The competition for actors in tragedy is introduced at the City Dionysia.

late 440s Sophocles' play *Ajax* is presented.

c. 445 The comic playwright Aristophanes is born.

443/2 Sophocles serves as *Hellenotamias* (treasurer of the Athenian empire). His position in public office reveals that he was not only a successful tragedian but also a politically active citizen.

442–40 Sophocles wins first prize with his production of *Antigone*. Such is the popularity of the play that Sophocles is elected general during an expedition against the island of Samos (Samian War, 440 BC), serving alongside Pericles.

438 Sophocles for the first time defeats the younger poet Euripides and is awarded first prize.

431–04 A less optimistic period begins, that of the Peloponnesian War and the gradual decline of the Athenian empire. During the second summer of the war, in a city overcrowded with refugees from the Spartan invasion, plague raged and persisted over the next few years. Pericles is believed to have been one of the victims (in 429). The events of the war must have inspired and influenced many of Sophocles' later plays.

late 430s During this period of change and uncertainty Sophocles' *Women of Trachis* is presented, perhaps the most Euripidean of his surviving plays.

mid 420s *Oedipus the King* is awarded second prize. Sophocles poses questions in the play regarding fate and personal choice, revealing a rather critical attitude towards the Athenian 'enlightment' (Pericles' golden years).

420/19 Sophocles becomes priest of the cult of the god Asclepios, or cult of the Healing Hero, showing that he was indeed a religious man. He is thought to have provided an altar for the god at his own home when the cult was first introduced to Athens until a proper public shrine could be built. Less certain is the belief that Sophocles himself was worshipped as a hero under the name Dexion (receiver of the god) after his death.

?415 In the later stages of his career his play *Electra* is presented, which again demonstrates the strong commitment of an unmarried heroine to her father (Agamemnon) and brother (Orestes).

415–13 Sicilian Expedition. The Athenians suffer total defeat in Sicily (413) and Sophocles is called to serve as *proboulos* (special state commissioner) in the emergency situation.

409 Sophocles wins first prize with his play *Philoctetes*.

406 Sophocles dies in Athens.

404 Peace between Athens and Sparta is signed. Rule of the Thirty Tyrants in Athens.

401 *Oedipus at Colonus* is produced posthumously by Sophocles' grandson, who is also a tragic poet. Due to its setting, Sophocles' birthplace, the play is believed to contain autobiographical elements.

Plot

Oedipus the King, following the formal conventions of Greek tragedy, is composed of six scenes (an opening scene [*prologos*], then, in this case, four scenes, followed by a final scene [*exodus*]), which are separated distinctly by five choral songs (opening lyric [*parodos*] and here, four choral songs [*stasima*]) which have some relevance to the dramatic situation.

The formality, cohesion and dramatic economy of the whole plot structure was not only second nature to the spectators and tragedians of ancient Greece but a significant component upon which the play's success depended. As Aristotle observed in his monumental work of literary criticism, *Poetics,* much of the excitement of a tragic performance comes from the skilful structuring of the plot (*muthos*). Aristotle's ideal plot structure was that of *Oedipus the King* because, according to him, the outcome of the play and emotive force of the tragedy depended principally on a tightly constructed cause-and-effect chain of actions instead of on the protagonist's character. Not one scene is superfluous. The successive circumstances of the play arise gradually and naturally one out of the other and are connected with such careful consideration that if the smallest part were taken away the whole play would collapse.

Opening scene (prologos)

The scene opens with a procession of suppliants, Theban citizens, carrying incense burners and garlanded laurel branches which they lay on the altar in the centre of the stage. When the crowd settles, Oedipus enters from the central door of the palace and is confronted by his people in their distress. The old priest of Zeus, who acts as spokesman for the crowd, describes the horrific situation in the city where people and animals are dying and appeals to Oedipus to solve the present mystery of the plague just as in the past he solved the riddle of the Sphinx and became king.

Oedipus' reply manifests a concern and anxiety for his people and informs the crowd of Creon's trip to Delphi to consult the oracle and learn what might be done to save the city. The priest announces Creon's arrival, perfectly on cue, with good news. In public, Creon gives a detailed report of Apollo's command to find the murderers of Laius and outlines the circumstances of his death. In response, Oedipus declares his readiness to follow the will of Apollo and avenge the crime. The scene ends with Oedipus entering the palace, and the suppliants removing their branches from the altar and exiting by the side entrance. The old priest suggests they pray to Apollo.

First choral song (parodos)
The chorus of the elders of Thebes enter by the side entrance chanting. In an emotional restatement of the central issue, they call on the gods, Athene, Artemis and Apollo, to save them in the battle against plague and destruction.

First scene (*first* epeisodion)
Oedipus enters from the palace to address the chorus, as if addressing the entire city. His first words establish an immediate connection with the first choral song by declaring that he will provide an answer to their prayer, reaffirming his desire to help. In a long monologue he demands that the murderer should give himself up and ends with a curse upon anyone, including himself, who shelters the criminal. Following Oedipus' speech, a dialogue with the chorus takes place in which the king's active concern to discover the truth is stressed. The chorus also suggest asking the assistance of the famous blind seer Teiresias, preparing the audience for his imminent arrival.

Teiresias' appearance by the side entrance is perfectly timed. He is guided by a boy in the traditional manner. Oedipus' greeting is respectful, crediting the blind seer with insight and placing himself and the city's rescue in the hands of the prophet.

To his surprise, Oedipus is met with dismay and resistance as Teiresias realises what he is being asked to disclose. Teiresias requests to be sent home and though the king and chorus beg him to stay, the seer persistently refuses to uncover the truth. As a result, Oedipus accuses Teiresias of complicity in the murder-plot against Laius, which prompts the prophet to reveal that Oedipus is the curse of his city. Oedipus in his anger forces the seer to repeat his accusation and Teiresias also points in veiled terms to Oedipus' incestuous marriage. Oedipus is convinced that he has fallen victim to a conspiracy planned by Creon and the prophet. The accusation is rebuked by Teiresias, who denounces Oedipus' blindness and warns him of the fate that awaits him. The scene ends on Teiresias' final speech in which he repeats his prophetic words and challenges Oedipus to solve this riddle as he did the Sphinx's. The boy leads him away.

Second choral song (*first* stasimon)
The chorus wonder about the identity of the murderer of whom Apollo speaks. In highly metaphorical terms they describe him as a hunted animal unable to escape the persecuting power of the god and his executioners. In the second part of the song, the chorus voice their uncertainty about Teiresias' prophecy as they cannot bring themselves to believe, without any evidence, that the saviour of this city, Oedipus, is the perpetrator of a crime.

Second scene (*second* epeisodion)
Following the choral song, Creon reappears on stage and in disbelief questions the chorus to establish the facts about the terrible charges that Oedipus has made against him.

Oedipus enters, directly accusing the 'offender'. The scene demonstrates Oedipus' delusion and passionate fury in the face of Creon's moderate argument in self-defence. It is Creon who has the last word before Oedipus' wife, Jocasta, intervenes when the quarrel is at its climax. The chorus begs Oedipus not to condemn Creon and Oedipus reiterates that in upholding Creon's innocence they are accusing himself of responsibility for Laius' murder. Grudgingly Oedipus merely banishes Creon.

Jocasta, who believes in her husband's innocence, tries to reassure Oedipus about the unreliability of oracles and seers. As an example she tells him how the oracle foretold to Laius that their child would kill him. She explains how this prophecy turned out to be false as Laius was killed by robbers at a crossroads, and the child perished in the mountains. Jocasta's story is based on the statement of the sole survivor of the incident, Laius' servant. In rising fear at Jocasta's description of the place where Laius was killed, Oedipus asks to meet the servant. He explains the reason for his anxiety to

Jocasta, telling her of the oracle he himself received in his youth at Delphi that he would kill his father and marry his mother, and going on to recount how he fled from his parents' home to avoid the prediction and killed some men in a quarrel at a crossroads. There is still one point which does not match his fears: Laius was reported to have been murdered by a group of men, providing Oedipus with hope, which is further encouraged by Jocasta. Jocasta is convinced that oracles are not trustworthy since Laius was not murdered by his son, as predicted. Oedipus nevertheless repeats his desire to see Laius' servant.

Third choral song (*second* stasimon)

The song's content is related to the preceding scene, with the chorus expressing their belief in justice and the laws of the gods. Without explicitly censuring Oedipus and Jocasta, they condemn a criminal and arrogant contempt for the gods and assert the traditional values of religion. They fear a general decline if rulers do not obey sacred laws and pray that the oracles of Laius may be fulfilled.

Third scene (*third* epeisodion)

In the third scene Jocasta enters the stage with her offerings of incense and garlands of flowers. As she voices a brief prayer to Apollo, the god whose oracle she has previously scorned, the women who escort her place her offerings on the altar.

Suddenly a messenger from Corinth enters, addressing the chorus and asking where he can find Oedipus. The man declares to Jocasta that Polybus is dead and that Oedipus is to be made king of Corinth. The queen, full of joy, calls for Oedipus whose fears will be removed by the news. Oedipus at first expresses delight at the news and scorn for the prophecy but then his fears return for the other part of it: that he will sleep with his mother. Jocasta's attempt to ease his mind is of no avail while the messenger's subsequent disclosure that Oedipus is not the true son of Polybus but was found on a mountainside makes things even worse. Jocasta is the first to realise the whole truth. She makes a desperate attempt to prevent Oedipus from seeking further information but he is too blind to see the obvious and persists with his search. Jocasta rushes from the scene with a cry of anguish, her last utterance. The scene ends with Oedipus restating his unalterable resolve to discover his origins.

Fourth choral song (*third* stasimon)
The chorus sing and dance an excited song, speculating about Oedipus' possibly divine descent.

Fourth scene (*fourth* epeisodion)
The scene opens with an old shepherd entering the stage escorted by palace servants. This former servant of Laius is confronted with the messenger, whom he had met in the mountains of Cithaeron at the time of Oedipus' exposure, and the whole truth is revealed. Oedipus in horror realises that the prophecy has been fulfilled.

Fifth choral song (*fourth* stasimon)
This song could be described as a lamentation for the fall of Oedipus where the destiny of a great king is presented as a universal example of man's uncertain and gloomy existence. It contrasts the heights of Oedipus' success with his extreme reversal of fortune and expresses the chorus' misery in the face of such an outcome.

Final scene (exodus)
The final scene opens with a messenger entering the stage from the palace, announcing to the chorus that terrible events have occurred and the queen is dead. He gives a graphic report of Jocasta's suicide and of how Oedipus has blinded himself. He then prepares the audience for Oedipus' arrival, which follows immediately. The chorus exclaim in horror at the sight of him. They concur with his reasoning and he answers their remark that he would be better dead than blinded by saying he could not have borne the sight of his parents in the underworld and death would not be punishment enough; he should never have survived his exposure on the mountainside. In a long monologue he displays the full measure of his misery.

In the final section Creon enters and treats Oedipus with decency and dignity. Oedipus asks to be sent away from Thebes and Creon replies that he must first consult the gods on this matter. Oedipus begs Creon to bury Jocasta, to let him die on the mountainside, and to let him say goodbye to his daughters. They arrive on stage before the tragic figure of their blinded father and he asks Creon to take care of them. There is a last small battle of wills between Oedipus and Creon when Oedipus wants to be sent away and Creon orders him into the palace. Oedipus learns to submit and the play concludes with the chorus underlining once again the unpredictability of human life.

Commentary

The myth

In classical Greece the plot and characters of a tragedy were not invented from scratch each time the writer composed a new play. Sophocles had at his disposal a number of well-known legends and narratives closely aligned to the main values of his culture. Images and stories inspired by myths were connected with every form of artistic expression and ceremonial ritual, proving that the Greeks were not only familiar with a great number of mythical stories, but also made use of them to define themselves in the world and communicate their specific cultural issues. The myths were malleable and allowed the writer to become inventive, composing versions that on many occasions had little to do with their oral or literary precedents. The myths could be described as the basic material, and characters were open to revision and invention with regard to characterisation, motivation, sequence of events or even location.

In tragic theatre, even though the stories were set in a distant Bronze Age, the characters were mentally close to the audience and shared the values of the democratic period in Athens. The mythic subject helped the writer retain critical distance, allowing his audience to judge current political or ideological issues in an objective manner. The geographical characteristics of the mythical location, which usually existed in reality, could also be used in the stories and affect the dramatic events of the play. For example, the real city of Thebes had seven gates and in *Antigone* fierce fighting takes place at the seven gates of the city. One should note, however, that a myth could not be completely overturned as it was also considered part of Greece's history. The two most significant myths that were used in most Greek tragedies and were also perceived as part of Greece's distant historical past were the Theban cycle with the events that surrounded the house of Laius, and the rival Trojan cycle with the events that concerned the house of King Agamemnon.

The story of *Oedipus the King* is part of the legend of the house of Laius, king of Thebes, which also became a source of inspiration for two other surviving tragedies by Sophocles, *Antigone* and *Oedipus at Colonus*. Even though the mythical sequence of events places Oedipus' story at the beginning, the chronology in which the tragedies were written does not follow this order as the plays were not composed with the intention of being part of a trilogy: *Antigone* was written first, *Oedipus the King* second and *Oedipus at Colonus* last.

The Theban saga of Laius and his children was one of the most popular in the Greek literary and iconographic tradition and although one can never be entirely sure of a myth's original version, one can give a broad outline of the most important points which would have been familiar to Sophocles' audience when *Oedipus* was first performed in the mid 420s BC. The myth runs as follows: Laius, king of Thebes, has been cursed by Apollo, protector of youth and boys, because the king had allegedly raped Pelops' son Chrysippus who then committed suicide from shame. The curse is to run for three generations: Laius, his son Oedipus and Oedipus' sons Eteocles and Polynices. Laius and his wife Jocasta receive a prophecy from Apollo's oracle that Oedipus will murder his father and marry his mother. Full of fear, they seek to defy the prophecy by leaving their infant to perish on a lonely mountainside. However they do not realise that he survives. In accordance with the prophecy, the infant grows and unknowingly kills his father Laius, and marries his mother Jocasta by whom he has four children, two sons, Eteocles and Polynices, and two daughters, Ismene and Antigone. *Oedipus the King* deals with Oedipus' discovery of the horrible truth and the tragic consequences that follow: Jocasta's suicide and Oedipus blinding himself.[1] According to the myth the latter eventually dies in exile. At some point during his life Oedipus curses his sons, pronouncing that they will kill each other. After Oedipus' death, Eteocles and Polynices agree that they will each rule Thebes as king in alternate years. During his time in exile, Polynices marries Argia, daughter of Adrastus, king of Argos. When after a year Eteocles refuses to abdicate, violating their original agreement, Polynices leads an army of Argives against Thebes to claim the throne for himself. A fierce battle ensues, after which the brothers

[1] In the *Odyssey* (XI.271–80) there is no suggestion that Oedipus blinded himself, as in Sophocles, while in Euripides' version of the same myth he was apparently blinded by Laius' henchmen.

meet and slay one another at the seventh gate of Thebes in accordance with their father's curse. With all male heirs of Laius dead, Creon, brother of Jocasta, takes over as king of Thebes and this is the point at which the story of Sophocles' *Antigone* begins.

In the next phase of the myth, which Sophocles did not deal with, Creon as ruler refuses to allow the Argives to recover their dead but is eventually compelled to change his mind through the intervention of Theseus and an Athenian army. At a later stage of the story the sons of the seven who died at the gates return to destroy Thebes.

A great number of important pre-Sophoclean literary versions dealt with the Theban saga, the most recent dramatic version to Sophocles' *Antigone* being Aechylus' trilogy *Laius*, *Oedipus* and the surviving tragedy *Seven Against Thebes*. Sophocles and his audience would have been fully conscious of these.

The festival

The tragedy of *Oedipus the King* was presented in the Theatre of Dionysus as part of a drama competition that took place every year during the City (or Great) Dionysia, one of the city's numerous festivals.

The City Dionysia, which was dedicated to Dionysus, god of fertility, wine and theatre, was one of Athens' greatest annual festivals and aimed to celebrate the god's arrival in Athens as well as the city's wealth and prosperity. The event took place in mid to late March when seagoing again became possible after the winter. This meant that it was easy for foreign guests to visit the city and witness the festive activities. Another significant aspect of the timing of the event was the fact that the military campaigns and election of the ten generals took place soon after it ended; indeed the drama competitions could have had a strong influence upon current political decisions. For example, it is claimed that Sophocles himself was elected general because of his success with *Antigone*.

The radical democracy of Athens was reflected in the overall organisation of the festival which was an inclusive and participatory event. Although it is difficult to determine the precise order of the activities, a rough schedule of the festival can be made as it developed until the outbreak of the Peloponnesian War in 431 BC.

The day before the official beginning of the City Dionysia a pre-contest took place during which the poets and their casts (out of costume) described the plays they were due to perform in the drama competitions. The audience therefore were already informed about what they were expected to view in the following days.

The next morning the first day of the festival began and all normal life came to a halt. The wooden statue of Dionysus was led into the city escorted by young men carrying lighted torches, in a ceremony which represented the god's arrival in Athens. At the end of the evening procession the statue was positioned in a temple below the theatre of Dionysus where it remained for the duration of the festival.

The second day a great civic procession took place in which each citizen showed his civic status by a specific costume while the foreign guests were identified by scarlet robes. The sponsors of the drama performances (*choregoi*) were also marked out by wearing rich gowns. During this procession all citizens were included, typical not only of a democratic society but also of many Dionysiac cults. The procession included a number of dances (*dithyrambs*) performed by each tribe of Athens, and ended with the sacrifice of bulls at the altar below the theatre.

On the third day, the drama competitions commenced between three tragic poets and five comic poets. Before they began a piglet was sacrificed and its dead body carried around the performance area to purify the space in which the plays would be staged. The decision about who was to compete was made by a state official (*archon*) selected by lot about six months in advance. The same person allocated each poet to a wealthy sponsor chosen by the state. The sponsor's responsibility was to finance the whole production and the training of the chorus, as a form of taxation.

The drama competitions lasted four days. Dramatists presented three tragedies, a 'satyr' play, and a comedy each day. Sophocles is sometimes held to have been the first to abandon the form of the trilogy (three tragedies) to tell a single story (Aeschylus' *Oresteia* is the only surviving example). Instead he made each tragedy a complete entity in itself. However some people believe that Aeschylus in fact was the first with his tragedy *Persians* in 472, also the first surviving play to have been inspired by real events. Prizes were awarded to the poets and the actors (from 449 BC onwards) at the end of the festival by ten judges (a representative from each tribe), elected on the opening day of the festival by lot and sworn to impartiality.

The religious and civic activities that surrounded the productions must have created part of the play's meaning. In ancient Greece the viewing of a tragedy or comedy was not only a form of entertainment and education but also a religious as well as a public experience, which added to the play a political dimension and ritual quality.

It is obvious that the choral odes, laments, prayers and supplications which so often take place in *Oedipus the King* would have had an extra meaning for an audience surrounded by sacrificial rites and religious dances. In the same way, the monologues of Oedipus in which he expresses his commitment to saving his city would probably have brought to mind the famous orations given by political personalities (e.g. Pericles) during the festival, in which they expressed their dedication and pride in their glorious city.

Finally, the competitive nature of the event would have added a playful element as many spectators would have supported and cheered for their favourite poet or actor, participating in this way in the whole process. The art of persuasion (rhetoric) as expressed in fifth-century public speeches (in the assembly, the law courts, etc.) was also present in the theatre, not only for performers in their roles but also as actors and dancers trying to convince their audience that their performance and play deserved the first prize.

In 449 the competition for actors in tragedy was introduced at the City Dionysia and the actor gradually became as important as the dramatist. It might well have affected the way in which actors delivered their parts or even the way in which parts were composed by the tragic poet. For example, Aeschylus' early plays were more chorus-oriented and affirming of socio-political values while Sophocles places more emphasis on the individual (the Sophoclean hero) and the issue of personal choice (see pp. xxx–xxxii and xxxvii–xxxviii).

Political context

Oedipus the King was presented around the time of the outbreak of the Peloponnesian War (*c.* 430 BC) and for some scholars (Knox, Wiles) the play itself would have had definite political overtones for an Athenian audience. The best source of information regarding the political events of the time is the account of the Peloponnesian War given by the historian Thucydides, writing at the time and renowned for his objectivity and scientific precision in describing the war and its causes.

Sparta had announced that she declared war against Athens, among other reasons, to liberate Greece from Athenian oppression. And with some justification, because Athens had converted the Delian League (founded in 477 as a defensive alliance against the Persians) into an Athenian empire, thus demonstrating the city's imperialistic tendencies. Initially the League's treasury was located on the island of Delos – hence the League's name – but Pericles transferred it to Athens, boosting the city's political and financial power and gradually transforming the federation into an Athenian superpower.

Following the outbreak of the war, the strategy of Pericles (the political leader of Athens), to survive the enemy's attacks, was to abandon the countryside to the Spartans and concentrate everyone in the city itself, which could receive supplies from across the sea. As long as Athens was free to strike from the sea against Sparta's coastal allies, it could create tensions within the Spartan alliance. In 431 and 430, the Spartans invaded the countryside of Athens and laid waste large parts of it while the Athenians retaliated with attacks on the Spartan navy. However, it soon became apparent that Pericles' strategy was too expensive and ambitious. Worse was to come, because in 429, a terrible plague broke out and in the cramped conditions of the city about a third of the Athenian citizens, including Pericles, perished. At the same time, the Spartans laid siege to Plataea, which fell in 427.

It is undeniable that in *Oedipus the King* there are echoes of current events in the Peloponnesian War, as it deals with the pressing issue of charismatic leadership (in Athens, Pericles) and the causes for its decline in an uncertain environment of devastation and disease. When approaching Oedipus as a political figure one can easily see a connection between the dramatic protagonist and the Athenian leader, with his imperialistic policies, undermined by the plague. The plague is also a central issue in *Oedipus the King* for it is the pollution of the city which leads to the protagonist's self-discovery and his tragic downfall.

When considering the political context in which the tragedy was presented one could approach the play as a political lesson for authoritarian and over-confident leaders, demonstrating through Oedipus' dramatic collapse that there is no place for one-man rule in a democratic world overseen by the gods. This raises the question, were Athens and Pericles, like the tragic protagonist in *Oedipus the King*, at their highest moment of greatness and arrogance when faced with a reversal of fortune through misreading the divine signals? Even the ultra-rational historian Thucydides in his account of the war has made Pericles refer to the plague as something 'heaven-sent' (*daimonia*) and beyond the power of mortals to deal with (Thuc. II.64.2.).

The performance

The theatrical space

Oedipus the King was first performed in the morning in the open-air Theatre of Dionysus, on the south-east slope of the Acropolis, just above the temple of Dionysus and close (on the other side of the Acropolis hill) to the market place (*agora*) where all political, judicial, commercial and religious activities took place, making it both metaphorically and literally the centre of the city.

The shape of the theatre itself developed according to the topography of the Acropolis hill. This meant that the hillside rising up from the temple of Dionysus gradually formed a natural theatre auditorium with the audience sitting initially on the ground and later on wooden planks. This offered spectators a better view than level ground, allowing them to look down on a performance area (*orchestra*) which gradually developed into a circle where the tragedies unfolded through the skilful acting and dancing of the performers.

A wooden structure, the stage building or *skene*, was positioned on the circular performance area. The front of the *skene* was dominated by a central door, marking the boundary between inner and outer space, private and public domain, and to a certain degree between female and male spheres. At a practical level it also served as the place where actors changed costumes and masks without being seen. The invention of *skenographia* (scene painting) is credited by Aristotle to Sophocles. The front of the *skene* was probably rendered to look like a palace, temple, etc., depending on the play's context.

Apart from the central door, the circular performance area had another two side-entrances from which the male characters usually arrived or departed. Women, as well as royal residents of the palace, usually used the main door.

Due to the open-air nature of the theatre it was impossible for the spectators to observe the play without taking into account their surroundings, including the temple of Dionysus, the Parthenon (temple of Athene) looming just behind them, the market on the other side of the slope, the rocky terrain, the city walls, the sea and sunny sky, which would have served as natural correlatives to the performer's words and actions. Equally, the entrances and exits would have been arranged to draw meaning from the topography of the theatre, with each side giving a different feel to the spectators. In most tragedies the right side is connected with the civilised and ordered world of the city and the left with the wilderness of the country. We must assume, for instance, that in *Oedipus the King*, Creon, on his first arrival, the Corinthian messenger and the shepherd all enter from the left side as they arrive from the country.

The actors

In ancient Greek theatre three professional male actors, the protagonist (first competitor), deuteragonist (second competitor), and tritagonist (third competitor), interpreted all the characters in the play, their status depending on the length and difficulty of their roles. The actors were assigned to the dramatist by the state official in charge of the festival, but on many occasions, the poet himself could also participate by playing the central part. It is important to note that the poet was not a simple dramatist but also functioned as the modern-day director, guiding and instructing his actors on how to perform their parts. According to Aristotle, Sophocles was the first dramatist to make use of a third speaker. However Aeschylus' *Oresteia* shows evidence of a third actor with Pylades in *Choephoroi*, who delivers a single line.

It is obvious that when two characters co-existed on stage the parts could not be interpreted by the same actor. With this in mind the most likely distribution in *Oedipus the King* would seem to be that the role of Oedipus would have been played by the protagonist since his part is longest and he appears on stage with all the other characters, while the two other actors would have played the rest of the dramatic roles.

Another interesting interpretation suggests that, rather than the protagonist being allotted a single role, the most demanding and challenging sections were distributed to the most talented and experienced performer.[1] This approach leans more on the necessity of skills when interpreting difficult and intense dramatic moments to produce a theatrically unifying quality to the production, and less on the modern Stanislavskian conception of the actor's need to interpret a single dramatic part in order to establish a psychological and intellectual connection with the character as it develops throughout the play. The characters are seen as physical entities that are complete only when realised in performance and not as dramatic entities that pre-exist in the words of the text.

The spectators would have witnessed a series of simple but well-constructed confrontations between two actors (Oedipus–Creon, Oedipus–Teiresias, Oedipus–Jocasta), but no special settings or props were required. However, the concentration on the crisis of a single individual and the static nature of the play (almost no action occurs until the suicide and self-mutilation at the end) also demanded an additional element produced by the presence of the third actor. Part of Sophocles' skills as a dramatist and theatre practitioner was the inclusion of dialogue between three characters that was used in successively more complex scenes (Creon–Oedipus–Jocasta, Messenger–Jocasta–Oedipus and the famous Oedipus–Messenger–Shepherd), generating triangular and more exciting patterns of speech. For example, as Knox argues, 'the frantic speed of the final revelation could not have been successful without the presence of the third actor'.[2]

But the power of masked acting must also be considered, as it was the configuration of the parts of the body, and one actor in relation to another or to the chorus, as well as the effectiveness of the speech, that dictated meaning and produced a sense of excitement. During the performance, the spectators looked down on three masked actors who wore colourful long robes (*chiton*), spoke clearly and moved in a stylised manner highlighting the ceremonial quality of the production. The usage of masks naturally facilitated the swift changes from one part to another, while at the same time helped to identify the gender and age of each character, especially for those viewing from a long distance. For example, female masks were paler than male since women had lighter skins because they spent most of their time indoors, while older males were distinguished from younger boys by facial hair.

[1] This interpretation seems more convincing for plays which have two central characters, such as *Antigone*, rather than for *Oedipus the King*.
[2] Knox, 1964, p.7.

Beyond these practical reasons, however, it is important to underline that in ancient Greece the use of the mask was not an exotic concept but a natural way of performing and its presence was perceived as a defining element of theatre, representing the loss of the actor's persona to the persona of the mythical character. Moreover, it determined the overall acting technique, as the movements and gestures of the performers required to be enhanced to make up for the lack of facial expression. The notion of psychological acting through the subtle variations of facial expression was alien to the ancient Greeks. Speech also became an important component of the performance as the masked and fully covered bodies naturally drove the audience's attention to the spoken words, which in conjunction with the formal figures and their spatial context produced theatrical meaning. Equally important to the direction of meaning was the presence and movement of the chorus with its various functions.

The chorus

The members of the chorus were selected by the Athenian community of citizens six to eight months in advance in order to start their demanding training. Although amateurs, they would still have been extremely skilful, due to their familiarity with and participation in other dances that were part of most ritual events of the city.

During the performance of *Oedipus the King* the members of the chorus abandoned their individuality to become a group of fifteen masked male dancers dressed in long robes. (Sophocles increased the number of the tragic chorus from twelve to fifteen.) These dancers represented a single organism which projected a single voice, the voice of the elders of Thebes.

The members of the chorus, with the accompaniment of the double-pipe player, were required to dance and sing in unison the lyrics of the play with clear articulation and precise movements, highlighting visually and verbally the events and words that were played out before them. The rhythm of the words must have guided their movements, while the various metres in which the lyrics were written must have assumed particular dance steps that pointed to familiar ritual practices, making them easily recognisable to the spectators. Thus, the choreography of the group was an essential component of the experience, producing theatrical meaning through dance. As Rush Rehm suggests:

> The precise nature of the dance of the chorus has been lost but we gain some insight from the content and substance of the songs, from representations of dancers on ancient vases and sculpture, and from the lyric metres themselves. It seems likely that the Greek chorus did not eschew mimetic and expressive movements. When they sang of the animal world and the forces of nature, there was a quality in the dance that reflected its power and beauty. When the lyric included threnodic elements and other aspects of mourning rites, or dealt with sacrifice, weddings, athletic contests, or military actions, we may be sure the dance drew on recognisable gestures and movements from those rituals and events. (Rehm, 1992, p. 54)

It is difficult to guess the exact formations that the chorus developed on stage but one can assume that the odd number of fifteen would have encouraged a split into sub-groups and would have generated a strategic position for the chorus leader whose key responsibility was to guide his fellow dancers.

The chorus's attitude would not necessarily have been that of Sophocles or the attitude he wished to instil in his audience, but their position between actors and audience gave them part of the nature of both. They might have commented or reflected on the confrontations of characters such as Oedipus and Creon, Oedipus and Teiresias, by division into semi-choruses and by corporate response to each speaker in turn, and it is highly unlikely that they would have stood and watched impassively. It is agreed by most practitioners and spectators, who have viewed the revival of an ancient chorus on stage, that their physical movements, far from detracting from the focus of attention, can actually confirm it. Moreover in the large open-air theatres such as the ancient Greek ones, the further away the audience sits, the greater the effect. It has also been suggested that in *Oedipus the King* the chorus act as a jury with the protagonist trying to convince them of the necessity of his actions.

In conclusion, the theatrical purpose of the chorus could be understood in many ways but one of its most important functions was its ability to enhance the audience's understanding of the play through their physical reaction to the actions and words of the central characters. The ever-present chorus could function as a second audience that, due to its closeness to the events and its strategic position between characters and spectators, was powerful enough to guide the latter on how to appreciate the various dramatic situations.

Aristotle and *Oedipus the King*

Before discussing the various modern interpretations of *Oedipus the King* it is essential to look at the most influential ancient study of Hellenic literature, the first attempt to define and distinguish between literary genres (tragedy, comedy, epic poetry), Aristotle's *Poetics*. Written *c.* 330 BC about half a century after the death of Sophocles, the treatise not only refers repeatedly to *Oedipus the King*,[1] but also considers it the perfect tragedy. Not surprisingly then, Aristotle's analysis of tragedy fits the play very accurately, especially with regard to plot and character, on which I shall concentrate (the remaining elements mentioned by Aristotle, in order of significance, are thought, diction, song and spectacle). Aristotle's ideas for the construction of the perfect tragedy in terms of plot and character are built around two crucial effects which, he says, bring about the audience's final 'purging' (*catharsis*). These are: 1) the arousal of fear for what might befall the hero; 2) the arousal of pity for the suffering hero after his downfall.

Plot (simple and complex)

For Aristotle the plot more than any other element determines the success and effectiveness of the play. He describes it as 'the soul of a tragedy'. Thus its tight structure, based on the law of probability, as well as its unity (a cause-and-effect chain of events), is most important for producing the emotions of pity and fear in the audience.

According to Aristotle, the plot of a tragedy could either be simple or complex, although complex is preferable. In simple plots

[1] Chapter 11 discusses reversal in the play and comments on the combined effect of reversal and recognition; chapter 14 discusses the importance of the tragedy's inner structure in arousing pity and fear in the spectator; chapter 15 discusses the element of the incredible in the play and how it is acceptable as it is outside the action of the drama; chapter 16 discusses the recognition scene which Aristotle considers the best to be found in tragedy; chapter 24 talks about how the hero's ignorance of the manner of Laius' death is unlikely but does not harm the tragedy's credibility as it lies outside the action of the play; chapter 26 argues that if *Oedipus* were as long as the *Iliad* it would lack unity.

there is only a 'change of fortune' (*catastrophe*) in the hero's life while in complex plots there is also 'reversal of the situation' (*peripeteia*) and 'recognition' (*anagnorisis*), both connected with the hero's catastrophe. Aristotle explains that 'reversal of the situation' occurs when a character's action produces the opposite effect to what was initially intended (tragic irony) and that 'recognition' signals a character's transition from ignorance to knowledge, affecting the relationship between the persons of the drama.

Aristotle states that 'the best form of recognition is coincident with a reversal of the situation, as in *Oedipus*'. In *Oedipus the King* the 'reversal of the situation' occurs through the Corinthian messenger's delivery of news. Although he seeks to reassure Oedipus with his announcement, in fact he causes a terrible revelation. The action of the messenger plays a pivotal part in the development of the play and is directly connected to Aristotle's concept of 'recognition' as it allows Oedipus to discover his true identity by obtaining the knowledge he has so far lacked. This causes the protagonist's 'change of fortune' from good to bad, bringing about the third and final part of the plot, 'the scene of suffering'.[1]

There are scholars (for instance, B. M. W. Knox) who contend that *Oedipus the King* does not fit the Aristotelian formula but rather that the play corresponds to Aristotle's description of what tragedy should avoid. They base their argument on Aristotle's preference in *Poetics*, 14, for the complex 'happy ending' in which *anagnorisis* and *peripeteia* together avert *pathos* (suffering), giving as an example Euripides' *Iphigeneia in Tauris*. *Anagnorisis* and *peripeteia* in this play prevent violent suffering rather than follow it. In *Oedipus the King*, on the other hand, revelation comes after the violent death of Laius and consequent suffering of the city and when it happens it causes the unhappy ending of a noble man.

[1] Arguably most of Oedipus' individual actions could be considered a 'reversal of the situation', providing him gradually with knowledge that will cause his final downfall. So 'recognition', as well as 'reversal', could be viewed as a recurrent pattern in the plot and not a single occurrence.

Character
Aristotle clearly states that character holds the second place in tragedy and its purpose is to support the plot rather than to instigate the actions. Thus, in Greek tragedy character depends on function and is determined by the hero's/heroine's behaviour and not by his/her inner self or soul as in most modern psychological dramas.

According to Aristotle, in a perfect tragedy character will support the plot while the person's motivations will be directly linked to the cause-and-effect chain of actions. Moreover, the character should be famous and prosperous in order for his 'change of fortune' to be from good to bad. Oedipus' nobility, virtue and intelligence, for example, form his first qualifications as a tragic hero as they generate the audience's respect for the hero, who must be viewed as a 'larger and better version of themselves', making his downfall much more effective.

The 'change of fortune' must come as a result of a mistake (*hamartia*). But this must not be misunderstood as a weakness of character but rather as a miscalculation in judgement. The term *hamartia* has been the subject of much debate, mainly generated by the way in which scholars have chosen to translate the Aristotelian term. The Greek word, typically translated as 'tragic flaw', is actually closer to 'mistake' or 'error'. Hence the 'change in fortune' is more probably connected to the protagonist's destructive actions taken in ignorance than to an inherent personality weakness, which would make the audience lose respect for him and be unable to pity him. In Oedipus' case his basic flaw, for which he is not responsible, is his ignorance of his identity. The audience fear for the hero as there is nothing he can do to change his tragic downfall.

Oedipus has often been described as the ideal tragic character for he fulfils the Aristotelian parameters that define the tragic hero. As Aristotle concludes when discussing the poet's aims with regard to character and plot construction:

> There remains, then, the character between these two extremes – that of a man who is not eminently good and just, yet whose misfortune is brought about not by vice or depravity, but by some error or frailty. He must be one who is highly renowned and prosperous – a personage like Oedipus, Thyestes, or other illustrious men of such families. (Aristotle, *Poetics*, 13, trans. S. H. Butcher, 4th ed., London, Macmillan, 1907)

Modern interpretations of *Oedipus the King*

One can never be sure of the original meaning of a play written to be staged two and a half thousand years ago or the way in which the original audience perceived the scenes and the tragedy as a whole. Such considerations will always remain speculative. Equally it is inevitable that the tragedy will yield different meanings for the spectators according to the context in which it is presented, or in the case of readers, the context of their study. However most critics agree that some interpretations and approaches are more convincing than others.

Twentieth-century scholars either attempt to discern a consistent moral universe by stressing the didactic nature of the play or, influenced by Aristotle's analysis of the tragedy (*Poetics,* chapter 6), value its emotive and involving force, created by an exciting and meticulously ordered plot-line (*muthos*) with all the flavour of a legal investigation. There is a search for evidence, cross-examination of witnesses, the passing of judgement and sentencing. There is even the inner audience, the chorus, before whom most of the cross-examinations occur, and to whose opinion the protagonist both refers and defers.

Approaching the tragedy as a didactic piece, one can either read it as an optimistic play in which a lesson is to be drawn about arrogant behaviour, or as a more pessimistic piece in which greatness of character is unfairly punished by the gods. Those who hold a moralistic view of the play consider the hero's fall to be a tragic consequence of his character and lack of moderation and expect the audience to disapprove of his over-confidence and disrespectful treatment of the prophet and Creon.

The second and more deterministic view, in contrast, holds that the fault lies with the gods and that Oedipus suffers unjustly. It has been argued that the problem with this approach is that Sophocles' heroes are not always entirely estimable and do in fact display some considerable faults of character. Freud, in his famous theory of the Oedipus complex, also takes the line that Sophocles depicted what was fated and not Oedipus' free moral choice.

> *Oedipus Rex* is what is known as a tragedy of destiny. Its tragic effect is said to lie in the contrast between the supreme will of the gods and the vain attempts of mankind to escape the evil that threatens them. The lesson which, it is said, the deeply moved spectator should learn

> from the tragedy is submission to the divine will and realisation of his own impotence. (Freud, 1966, p. 102)

The Freudian interpretation suggested that the play had a universal rather than culturally specific significance as it acted out the inner and unconscious desires within every individual as well as the breaching of fundamental taboos:

> His [Oedipus'] destiny moves us only because it might have been ours – because the oracle laid the same curse upon us before our birth as upon him. It is the fate of all of us, perhaps, to direct our first sexual impulse towards our mother and our first hatred and our first murderous wish against our father. (Ibid., p. 103)[1]

Attention is thus focused on the solitary, larger-than-life hero, whose fate alone concerns the reader or audience.

According to Storey and Allan, a more recent trend has been to consider the world of Sophocles 'as profoundly disturbing, without committing oneself either to divine providence or to human excellence' (Storey and Allan, 2005, p. 128). For Vernant, the character of Oedipus is an ambiguous figure, 'a problem, a riddle', impossible for the audience to describe or define, due to his double identity as 'tyrant' (*tyrannos*), the greatest of all, and 'polluter' (*pharmakos*), the lowest of all (Vernant, 1988, pp. 113–40). Thus, the play offers neither a psychological nor determinist view of life but a structure of ambiguity and reversal which reflects the duality of the human condition and which, just like the riddle, challenges the possibility of exhaustive interpretations.

It is true that by approaching the play purely as a 'tragedy of fate' or 'a tragedy of free-will' one oversimplifies the dialectics and dynamics of the negotiations between characters, action and moral responsibility. Disregarding one element in favour of another may well cause a superficial and one-sided reading of the play. It is the perfectly ordered and exciting accumulation of past incidents that build up a picture of Oedipus' heroic personality and degraded condition. In the same way it is the character of the hero in combination with his polluted state that brings about his downfall. His god-ordained destiny cannot be fulfilled without the meticulous and agonisingly slow unravelling of facts and without his intelligence and curiosity as a human being.

[1] It is interesting to note that Jocasta, in her speech on p. 36, specifically says, in advance of Freud, that it is every man's dream to marry his mother.

Finally, an aspect of the play which has been somewhat obscured in our post-Freudian era, when the urge to identify with the individual hero has become endemic, is its political aspect and the tension between charismatic leadership and excessive arrogance. In this interpretation, the tragedy is taken as a counterpoint to fifth-century Athenian democracy and the community spirit. As Wiles argues, *Oedipus the King* 'becomes a political play when we focus on the interaction of actor and chorus, and see how the chorus form a democratic mass jury' (Wiles, 2000, p. 62).

The characters

It is impossible to evaluate a character from Greek tragedy in purely psychological terms since Athenian drama does not offer the same details and depth of characterisation to be found in the plays of, for example, Ibsen. The internal psychological states remain largely unformulated by the text. Even though Sophocles' characters achieve a degree of coherence and distinctiveness that encourages the spectator or reader to begin to respond to them as if they were real persons, their essential qualities and characteristics derive either from their typical heroic status or seem defined by their precise social roles.

The central character as hero and scapegoat

All of Sophocles' dramas portray an important and charismatic central character around whom the tragedy unfolds and who could be described as isolated, set apart from his/her 'normal' fellow humans. In *Oedipus the King* the central character is Oedipus and the entire action comes as a result of his powerful will to discover the truth and save his city. His characteristics match those of the Sophoclean hero as described by the critic B. M. W. Knox in his famous study, *The Heroic Temper*.

According to Knox, the Sophoclean hero could be seen as a character who in the face of human opposition, makes a decision which derives from his individual nature, and then passionately maintains that decision even to the point of self-destruction. The hero decides against compromise as he refuses to yield; remains true to himself and his 'nature', which he inherited from his parents and which is his identity. Thus the heroic qualities include stubbornness, outspokenness and, above all, courage.

In *Oedipus the King* it is clear that the hero is faced with opposition in the explicit warnings of Teiresias, Jocasta's pleas to desist from his search, and the agonised begging of the shepherd at the very last moment. Oedipus however holds firm against the pressure. He is stubborn, self-willed, insisting throughout the play on his own way and on his rightness. From this resolution stems the dramatic tension of the tragedy. The hope that time will teach the hero is never fulfilled; he remains unchanged. Even when he realises that he has been unjust to Creon:

> . . . There is nothing I can say
> To him, and why should he listen to anything
> I say? I treated him unjustly. (p. 51)

he, nevertheless, remains the same man as he was at the start, trying to exert his own will:

> The children?
> Don't take them away from me! Don't do that! (p. 55)

He even needs to be reminded by Creon in the final moments of the play that he is no longer king. Creon's words show Oedipus' overall mentality and how his situation has changed:

> Don't give me orders! Those days are over.
> Your orders have brought you to this.
> Now you must learn to obey. (p. 55)

But as Knox argues, in Sophocles' tragedies 'it is through this refusal to accept human limitations that humanity achieves its true greatness. It is a greatness achieved not with the help and encouragement of the gods, but through the hero's loyalty to his nature in trial, suffering, and death' (Knox, 1964, p. 27).

It has also been suggested, however, that there is another side to Oedipus' character which is beyond his control, adding an ambiguous and enigmatic dimension to his figure. This, according to Vernant, is his dual role as hero and polluter of the city. His typical status as mythic hero has been repeatedly stressed in recent scholarship but 'the other, complementary and opposed side of Oedipus, has not been so clearly noted by the commentators' (Vernant, 1988, p. 115). Approaching the figure of Oedipus as a 'source of pollution', the ritual and religious dimensions of the play instantly become apparent. The polarity between heroic king and scapegoat is not something that was invented by Sophocles; it was already part of Athenian religious and political practice as well as social thought. It was common practice, for example, annually to purge all the pollution of the city accumulated over the year by parading and expelling criminals whose condition marked them out as inferior beings (the ritual of *Thargelia*). Similarly people of excessive virtue or political skill were unacceptable. The introduction of ostracism, the expulsion of the best, secured the continuation of democracy in Athens. In *Oedipus the King*, the protagonist's dual role as criminal and charismatic leader is typical of this.[1]

The supporting characters

Oedipus' powerful personality is not only realised through his persistent quest for the truth but also through his confrontations with the other less important members of the community. A series of encounters with conflicting personalities builds towards the slow accumulation of the facts that lead to the truth and Oedipus' final downfall.

To start with, there is the prophet Teiresias who represents the divine powers and underlines that there are realms of existence that are not subject to control. Oedipus' disrespect for him amounts to disrespect for the gods but it is through his presence that Oedipus' decision to search for his true identity is triggered. Oedipus and Teiresias complement one another: one physically blind but able to see the truth, the other sighted but blind to the truth. Together they demonstrate the imperfection and ambiguity of all human truth. Teresias is a servant of Apollo but, like Oedipus, he is caught up in an all-too-human anger. Initially he comes in obedience to Oedipus' summons but he will not disclose the truth. When forced to speak he speaks in riddles, concealing as much as he reveals.

Creon, in contrast, seems the voice of reason with his mild and

[1] Ostracism was an institution introduced in Athens after the overthrow of the tyranny of Peisistratos and his sons (510 BC) in order to secure democracy. It ordained that each Athenian citizen should write the name on an 'ostrake' (sea-shell) of whoever in his opinion held the greatest power to destroy democracy. The man who received the largest number of nominations (at least 6,000 ostraka) was then exiled for ten years. The law was passed, not to punish wrongdoing, but in order to prevent, through exile, those who had risen too high by virtue and popularity from becoming tyrants.

submissive nature, suited to his position in the royal palace, second-in-command. He is content with his political status and the prospect of ruling the city is not only something he has never contemplated but also something that he would not enjoy:

> As I ask myself, whether any sane man
> Would willingly exchange a quiet life
> Within the ruling family, for the wear and tear,
> The gruelling responsibility of government? (p. 23)

Creon's lack of ambition, reasonable arguments and moderate nature highlight even more Oedipus' passionate personality, extreme temper and irrational behaviour, turning him in many instances into an unsympathetic figure for the audience. The generous and forgiving nature of Creon, which is stressed towards the end of the play, secures his comeuppance in a reversal of fortune. The very accusation Oedipus made against Creon before is now applicable to himself. Creon may not be as charismatic as Oedipus but he is presented as a dignified person who is meticulous and respectful towards the gods.

Jocasta, on the other hand, is not respectful; she is a personification of the intellectual revolution of the fifth-century Athenian enlightenment, characterised by its scepticism about the existence of the gods. An example of this was the thinker Protagoras who declared that 'man is the measure of all things', challenging the power of the gods and their ability to affect human lives. Jocasta's belief in human progress through rational thinking is clear when she tries to reassure the king about the unreliability of oracles:

> That is how much oracles are worth. In future
> Whatever they say one way or the other
> I won't waste my time with any of them! (p. 32)

Her worldly sophisticated nature is also apparent:

> Live! Enjoy life. Take each day as it comes!
> As for marrying your mother, you're not the first to have dreamed that dream. (p. 36)

The remaining characters (Priest of Zeus, Messenger, Shepherd, Corinthian) have some personal characteristics to make them credible human beings (the Corinthian is a humorous buffoon) but more essentially they contribute to the meaning of the play by instigating a series of reactions from Oedipus, encouraging the spectators to appreciate the protagonist's nature and principles more fully, while advancing his discovery of the truth through the graphic presentation of the city's present situation (the priest) and the agonisingly slow unravelling of the protagonist's past (the messengers and shepherd).

The chorus

Unlike the chorus in *Antigone*, the Theban citizens in *Oedipus the King* are active participants in the play through their role as advisers to the king, initiated by their strong dedication both to him and to their city. The chorus's portrayal as responsible leaders and representatives of the citizens is further enhanced in the first choral song in which they call on the gods to help in a battle against the plague. Here they are far from passive survivors, resembling those who in a military crisis would be responsible for raising the troops for battle and assisting at the preliminary prayers. In their exchanges with Oedipus, their advice is earnestly given and respectfully considered, revealing a consultative relationship between the concerned leader and his counsellors, in a joint effort to search for answers. It is the chorus's dramatic function as advisers that gives them the opportunity to assist in the progression of the drama.

In their songs they tend to be cautious. They avoid speculation in favour of proof and individual personal matters in favour of those which concern the well-being of the city. Their advice following the confrontation between Creon and Oedipus displays to the full the chorus's reliance on reason and common sense. They avoid accusing their king of arrogance and hubristic behaviour, demonstrating their loyalty and their focus on the collective problems of the city. However their independent attitude is clearly apparent in their song following Jocasta's demonstration of the unreliability of oracles, when they are shocked by her impious attitude. The poet uses their sensible nature to show up, by contrast, aspects of the protagonist's personality. The chorus are not inferior to their king but their difference helps to define Oedipus' character in a way which is vital to the development of the plot.

Equally important is their function as the representative body of the city, for they highlight the political aspect of the play and

Oedipus' figure as political leader. The chorus respect their king and in return Oedipus honours their advice, notably in the matter of Creon's alleged betrayal. At their pleading he is prepared to spare Creon. The chorus, as responsible and loyal citizens, never stop reminding both Oedipus and the audience that the priority of a good citizen must always be the welfare of his state. Continually calling on the gods for help, they also set an example, in contrast to their king and queen, of respect for the gods and the old standards and values.

Central themes

There has been continuous debate about the nature of *Oedipus the King* and whether the play should be read as a religious ritual of reversal and purgation or as a humanist tragedy of error of judgement and misconduct arising from the hero's faulty character (see pp. xxviii–xxx). Those who approach the play from the religious point of view stress the role of external forces in the tragedy (curse, oracles) and their strong impact on the development of the action. Furthermore, its structure and presentation underline the idea of reversal as a religious ritual. On the other side, those who approach the play from a humanist angle consider the character's intelligence and morality as the key determinants in the unfolding of events and discovery of the truth. For them, Oedipus' heroic character is primarily responsible for his tragic downfall. Finally, a political approach considers Oedipus' behaviour and overall attitude towards his responsibilities and citizens, in order to establish whether the quality of his leadership and exceptional nature as an individual has caused his downfall.

Although in each interpretation primacy is given to a different set of themes, it is important to note that all issues (divine law, fate, human will, morality, politics) are not exclusive or irreconcilable as they all develop a dynamic and interdependent relationship which throws light on the meaning of the tragedy.

Religion, ritual and divine law (Oedipus as a source of pollution)

In no other extant plays of Sophocles does the action open with an elaborate public rite of supplication, setting the religious tone of the play. It also introduces the pattern of ritual which runs all through the play and contains a series of reversals in the protagonist's mental, physical and social condition. From being the recipient of prayers and lamentation at the prologue, he becomes the subject of those prayers and lamentations in the end.

The play opens with a graphic description of the situation in the city. The plague has emptied the 'courtyards Cadmus built', and the reason is straightforward, as Creon declares when reporting the oracle's instructions:

There is something unclean in our city.
Born here. Living here. It pollutes everything.
We harbour it. We must drive it out. (p. 8)

The language of the oracle, who acts as a mediator between the divine and the human, is clear:

It was bloodshed, the oracle says,
That whipped up this storm that's destroying us.

However, incest in the royal house, the disruption of fundamental taboos, is also a major reversal of the human and natural orders, something unclean. In the imagery of the first choral song the disruption is reflected in a description of violent outside forces, which penetrate the city's boundaries.

When the plague enforced its reign of terror
And a fire consumed us that no man could master.
Our agonies are beyond telling,
A whole city slowly dying
From an enemy no man can fight. [. . .]
Now let the bloodstained god of war
Whose savage music I hear
Though no swords clash or shields ring,
Be driven from our city. (p. 10)

The violation of primal religious codes has caused the fury of the divine forces, with catastrophic consequences for the city of Thebes, and it is only through the expulsion of the 'contaminator' that order can be restored. Oedipus' central role in the cleansing of the city is fundamental, for he is, according to the prophet Teiresias, the single source and cause of the disease.

You are the man: the unclean thing:
The dirt that breeds disease. (p. 16)

What he has done unknowingly and with no criminal intent is in fact the most horrific crime against the sacred order of things and the hero is guilty and soiled from the point of view of religion. Thus, through a divine curse (a typical way of singling out heroes in ancient Greek mythology) the protagonist finds himself cut off from the rest of the community, an outcast, feared, a figure with more than human qualities.

Although one could argue that the play shows a certain amount of scepticism about the validity of religious belief and oracular prophecies through the attitude of the queen, its tragic ending also raises the question of whether man is able to escape his destiny. Without suggesting that the actions of the central character are totally determined by external forces, religion and the idea of divine intervention are still essential elements in the tragedy. Whether Oedipus is driven to his end because he consciously dared to question and accuse Teiresias, mouthpiece of the gods, or because he unknowingly committed a sacred crime, the issues of faith and divine justice are fundamental as they appear at least partially to determine the severity of his crimes and punishment in his own view and in the view of his fellow citizens:

> OEDIPUS. Apollo, my friends, Apollo the god,
> His power determined my agony!
> But these eyes were blinded by my own hand.
> Why have eyes to see
> My own degradation and misery?
> CHORUS. This is the truth: simple and hard. (p. 48)

Heroic humanism and free will (Oedipus as a man of action and free agent)

Though destiny, fate and the will of the gods do indeed loom behind human action in the tragedy, that action does not merely reflect the whims of malicious deities. The divine voice in the play is the oracle of Apollo and the prophet Teiresias, who are both human agents of the gods and thus susceptible to error. As Jocasta points out,

> No one can forecast the future. I know
> What I am talking about, from personal experience. (p. 27)

When one considers the context in which the play was presented, where belief in prophecy and with it belief in the religious tradition as a whole was under attack, the argument which sees a sceptical attitude in the play becomes even stronger.

Oedipus is clearly an intelligent man of action. He is the investigator, prosecutor and judge of a murderer. His speeches are full of words, phrases and attitudes that link him to the intellectual enlightenment of Athens. There are of course factors in his life that no human force can alter but the hero's will appears as independent. Oedipus is a free agent and he is responsible to a great degree for his final catastrophe, since the plot does not consist of the actions which were predicted but of the process of his discovery that he has already fulfilled the prediction. And this discovery is entirely due to the course of action triggered by his heroic character. First of all, he sends Creon to Delphi to see what can be done to save the city. Then he chooses to undertake a vigorous public inquiry into the murder of Laius:

> We'll shine a fresh light into every corner
> Of the whole dark and musty business.
> [. . .] I am determined
> To do everything I can to help our city
> And show the god's justice. It's in my interest too
> To avenge this crime. (p. 9)

He is the driving force, who, despite the warnings of Teiresias, the dissuasion of the queen and the supplication of the shepherd, pushes on towards the unveiling of the truth.

The question of responsibility for what happened before the play begins is obscured but the protagonist's personal responsibility for discovering that he has fulfilled his predicted destiny is evident. And this is why the figure of Oedipus succeeds in arousing our admiration and sympathy. The hero who, in his intelligence, commitment, courage and defiance represents humanity at its best, chooses to discover a truth which brings about his fall, reducing him from a great man, 'the best of men' in the words of the chorus (p. 6), to nothing. In his search he becomes a heroic example of man's commitment to find out his identity, his place and purpose in the world.

Politics (Oedipus and the polis)

The issue of politics is central to the play for Oedipus is above all, as its title suggests, a leader. The Greek title of the tragedy is *Oedipus Tyrannos* but *tyrannos* has an ambiguous meaning in Greek. A tyrant could either be bad (a despotic ruler) or good (a popular and charismatic leader), but in either case he is an absolute ruler who has not inherited his power but who has succeeded by intelligence, force and influence, as Oedipus has.

The centrality of Oedipus' political status and dedication to the interests of his city are evident throughout the play and are crucial in leading him to the discovery of the truth. Characteristic of his democratic attitude as a ruler is his rejection of Creon's hint that the answer concerning the pollution of the city should be kept private and under wraps.

> CREON. Do you want me to say it all here, in public,
> Or shall we go in?
> OEDIPUS. In public of course!
> While these people suffer, I suffer too.
> Their life concerns me, more than my own! (pp. 7–8)

The chorus also appear to respect their king. Throughout the course of the play this group of Theban elders present the public aspect of the story, stressing Oedipus' achievements as a man and his actions as a benefactor of the city. Notably, they never directly accuse their leader of arrogance or oppression, revealing a relationship of mutual respect.

> Oedipus saved our state;
> He publicly outwitted the Sphinx. Like gold,
> He was tested and found true. (p. 21)

Their attitude is not one of fear and religious awe, but of trust in a great statesman.

> We need
> Your help and guidance. We all remember
> How like a pilot in that desperate storm,
> Half-wrecked, you navigated us to harbour.
> You are our captain, in rough weather or calm. (p. 27)

Oedipus might display elements of arrogance and aggression towards some of the characters of the play (Teiresias, Creon, the Shepherd), indicating at times an authoritarian attitude, but never does he doubt the views and judgement of his people, who are represented through the presence and actions of the chorus. If

Oedipus becomes a tyrant in the negative meaning of the term, it is not because he has stopped caring for his people but rather because he has become obsessed with discovering his own identity. This leads him to an aggressive and forceful response. It is the duty of the citizens at this stage of the play, when Oedipus' priorities shift from public responsibility to his private fate, to remind their king of the devastating consequences for the state.

> Our city is in anguish. What greater blow
> Could fall on us in our misery
> Than anger and hatred between you two? (p. 26)

The words of the chorus in their cryptic central ode demonstrate the play's concern with the psychology of a tyrant:

> Arrogant self-love breeds absolute rule,
> The tyrant, who eats up money and men.
> He seeks absolute power
> And in one foolish hour
> Overreaches himself, and ends in the gutter. (p. 33)

Oedipus' increasing self-obsession, in combination with the final revelation of the truth, has clear political implications. There is no longer room in a democratic society for a figure such as him. The unstable meaning of the word tyrant is the best expression of Oedipus' mental state as he is gradually in danger of changing from being a popular leader into becoming an abusive despot.

Modern reception of *Oedipus the King*

There is always a production of *Oedipus the King* being staged in some part of the world; there are countless interpretations of the original text (by Corneille, Voltaire, von Kleist, Gide, Cocteau, Shelley, Yeats, etc.) and presentations of the tragedy on stage, film and television (Reinhardt, Guthrie, Pasolini, etc.).

The number of revivals and adaptations of *Oedipus the King* makes it impossible to cover the entire modern reception of the tragedy so I have chosen to focus on a few of the most significant. At this point it is worth noting that most theatre practitioners and film-makers have tended to read the play as a tragedy of the individual, in which the incestuous nature of the protagonist's crime is stressed at the expense of the political side of the play. This is not unrelated to the emergence of Freud's theory of the Oedipus complex at the turn of the twentieth century, which has strongly determined most modern adaptations of Sophocles' tragedy.

'Oedipus the King' on the late nineteenth- and early twentieth-century European stage

Freud's famous theory was perhaps even influenced by the theatre of his time. One of the most significant productions of the nineteenth century, which Freud himself attended, occurred in France in 1881, in a rhymed translation by Jules Lacroix. The leading actor, Mounet-Sully, achieved an overwhelming success, turning the production into an international triumph. What astonished the viewers most was the protagonist's ability to convey in an extremely powerful and highly physical manner Oedipus' fear and pain, particularly after his self-mutilation. The production's concentration on the emotions of a single character were further enhanced by the nature of the theatrical space, in combination with the lighting. The proscenium stage isolated the hero from the viewers, who sat in a darkened auditorium while the footlights amplified his features, allowing the spectators to identify more effectively with the mythic figure. In contrast, the chorus's part was diminished, with the group of Theban elders adopting a purely decorative role.

At the same time, in Victorian England, all productions based on the *Oedipus* story were censored on the grounds that it was impossible to present a tragedy dealing with incest and parricide. Despite the efforts of a number of intellectuals to abolish this kind of theatre censorship, it took a long time for the tragedy to appear on the professional British stage. *Oedipus the King* was eventually presented in London thanks to the efforts of the classicist and translator Gilbert Murray, the theatre practitioner Harley Granville-Barker and most significantly the famous production by Max Reinhardt that became an inspiring force for both men. The Reinhardt production in Hugo von Hofmannsthal's version, first opened in Munich in 1910 and such was its popularity and success that it went on to be performed in almost every major city in Europe. In contrast to the Mounet-Sully production, Reinhardt chose to stress the Theban context of the play, but not in order to highlight its political side. His intention was rather to underline the individual suffering of Oedipus against a background of the community, stressing the isolated mental condition of the hero. The director, famous for his use of crowd scenes, employed around three hundred extras to represent the citizens of Thebes, plus a chorus of twenty-seven members, producing a monumental effect on the audience. The entrance of the suppliants at the beginning of the play was particularly striking as they surged through the auditorium. The large group eventually settled on a specially designated space, the steps at the front of the palace. Reinhardt's production was presented in England (with only a few alterations) in January 1912, using Murray's popular translation. The leading actor, Martin Harvey, was highly praised for his interpretation, and credited with being a great Oedipus.

Another production worth mentioning, due to the popularity of Yeats's version of the tragedy, was one which opened in Dublin in 1926 at the Abbey Theatre. In Yeats's version, and in its stage presentation, the chorus's role was almost obliterated, consisting now of only six members, and stressing once again Oedipus' status as the modern tragic hero.

'Oedipus the King' on the post-war global stage

Yeats's version was used in a number of significant post-war productions, highlighting the fact that Oedipus was still regarded and staged as the isolated hero whose political essence was of minor importance. Just after the war, in 1945, there was a London production at the Old Vic, directed by Michel Saint-Denis, with Laurence Olivier in the leading role. The latter's acclaimed performance was to go down in history as one of the most passionate and effective interpretations of the scene that follows the hero's discovery of the horrific truth.

In 1955, the Irish director Tyrone Guthrie also presented *Oedipus the King* using Yeats's version, as part of the New Shakespeare Festival in Ontario. Guthrie's approach was greatly influenced by the translator's ideas about the Greek hero. In the production, the character of Oedipus was no longer merely a man but became a symbolic figure of universal significance, stressed by the use of a larger-than-life golden mask which reinforced his mythic status. Guthrie's interpretation read the tragedy as a solemn sacrificial ceremony in which the masks served to obliterate the individual characteristics of the performers. The masked performance was a landmark not only because it presented a new interpretation which relied on the ritual elements of the play but most importantly because it became the first production to be filmed (1956), expanding the tragedy's popularity beyond Europe.

Peter Hall's much more recent *Oedipus* also stressed the ritual dimension of the play through the use of masks and formality in movement. It opened at the Olivier Theatre in 1996 and focused on the suffering and lonely journey of the individual, placing Oedipus on a projecting platform above the level of the chorus. There was no desire to stress the political aspect of the play, with the chorus representing a helpless and passive group of people similar to the suppliants who open the tragedy. The director, by choosing to use a mixture of male and female performers, distanced their role from that of the Sophoclean chorus who acted as elders and advisers.

'Oedipus the King' in film and television

The media of film and television have brought Sophocles' *Oedipus the King* to the attention of a wider audience. A typical example is the famous cinematic adaptation by the Italian director Pier Paolo Pasolini which made the tragedy popular through its atmospheric direction and deeply Freudian interpretation of the hero. The film, which has a prologue set in modern Italy, gives a Freudian account of the baby's birth, underlining the mother's caring attention and the father's rather distant and aggressive tendencies. The epilogue alludes to the final part of Sophocles' Theban saga, *Oedipus at Colonus*, showing the figure of a blind Oedipus wandering without purpose, led by a servant. The central section, which is filmed in an exotic landscape (a desert in Morocco) representing a desolate mythical past, includes both the mythic events which preceded Sophocles' play as well as a faithful enactment of Sophocles' version. Pasolini obliterates Oedipus' intellectual strength, presenting a character who is purely impulsive and highly unreasonable. The brutality and forceful nature of the hero is particularly stressed in the scene where he kills his real father.

Television is also a very effective medium for the presentation of Greek tragedy, not only because of its infinite directorial possibilities but also because it allows a wider audience to experience and familiarise themselves with the Greek masterpieces. The BBC televised version of *Oedipus the King* in Don Taylor's translation is still a highly moving production due to its strong cast, including famous names such as John Gielgud, who offer the viewer a sense of the tragedy's dramatic quality and intensity of feeling. The production aimed to make the play convincing and pleasurable for all those scholars 'who have spent a life studying the texts' but at the same time a thrilling experience for those who had never before heard of Greek drama. The version once again highlighted the sufferings of the individual hero who has been destroyed 'by circumstances and his own best and worst qualities, all working together'. As Don Taylor observed when discussing the quality of Sophocles' tragedies and their relevance to the lonely ordeals of modern heroes,

> Sophocles would have recognised in Salvador Allende and Leon Trotsky the materials for his kind of tragedy, and looking at our world, would have been quite sure that his Olympians are not dead. They have changed their names, and their instruments of action have changed with the times; but chance, arrogance, greed and the lust for power are still with us, and economic and political necessities construct traps for men and women as intricate as anything Apollo devised for Oedipus. (*Sophocles: Plays One*, p. xlvi)

The nature of the translation, as one will observe when reading this volume, reflects the fact that it was made for TV and for this reason had to exclude or at least keep to the minimum the poetic quality of the words spoken by Sophocles' characters. Don Taylor admitted that it was impossible to use any existing translation of the time, however effective, in television. Television by its nature demanded a more lively language. As he stated,

> Though television is a good medium for genuine dramatic poetry it is merciless with any kind of stilted language, and it soon became clear to us that we could present none of the existing translations of the Sophoclean trilogy with the faintest chance of the particular kind of success we hoped for. (Translator's note, p. liv)

Don Taylor's translation suited the production and fulfilled his aim of making a popular version that seemed to have been written 'not 2,500 years ago, but the day before yesterday, today and tomorrow'.

From these examples of productions and adaptations it is obvious that Greek tragedies will never be exhausted provided that artists and audiences use their creativity and enthusiasm to discover and yield their potential meanings. Whether the classical Greek masterpieces that were once performed in the ancient theatre of

Dionysus will remain alive depends not so much on academic and scholarly study of the texts as on the desire of the public to find ways in which tragedy can speak to their lives and hearts in the present.[1]

[1] For more on the adaptations and revivals mentioned in this section, see P. Burian, 'Tragedy Adapted for Stages and Screens: the Renaissance to the Present', pp. 253, 283, F. Macintosh, 'Tragedy in Performance: Nineteenth- and Twentieth-Century Productions', pp. 284–8, in Easterling, 1997, and Wiles, 2000, pp. 62–5.

Further Reading

The Greek text

The 'Oedipus Tyrannus' of Sophocles, ed. and trans. R. Jebb, Cambridge, CUP, 1958

The Plays of Sophocles, Commentaries IV: 'Oedipus Tyrannus', ed. and trans. J. C. Kamerbeek, Leiden, Brill, 1967

Sophoclis Fabulae, ed. H. Lloyd-Jones and N. G. Wilson, Oxford, OUP, 1990 (Greek text only)

Sophocles, ed. and trans. H. Lloyd-Jones, 3 vols, Cambridge MA, Harvard University Press (Greek text, facing English translation, introduction and notes)

Selected translations of Sophocles in English

Sophocles: Plays One, Methuen, London, 1986 (includes *Oedipus the King*, *Oedipus at Colonus*, *Antigone*)

Sophocles: Plays Two, Methuen, London, 1990 (includes *Ajax*, *Women of Trachis*, *Electra*, *Philoctetes*)

Sophocles: *'Antigone', 'Oedipus' and 'Electra'*, trans. H. D. F. Kitto, Oxford, OUP, 1998

Sophocles: *The Three Theban Plays*, trans. R. Fagles, Harmondsworth, Penguin, 1984

Greek theatre and drama

Allan, A. and Storey, Ian C. (eds), *A Guide to Ancient Greek Drama*, Oxford, Blackwell, 2005

Arnott, P. D., *Public and Performance in the Greek Theatre*, London, Routledge, 1989

Aylen, Leo, *The Greek Theatre*, New Jersey, Associated University Press, 1985

Bieber, M., *The Greek and Roman Theatre*, Princeton, Princeton University Press, 1961

Csapo, E. and Slater, W. J., *The Context of Ancient Drama*, Ann

Arbor, University of Michigan Press, 1995

Easterling, P. E. (ed.), *Cambridge Companion to Greek Tragedy*, Cambridge, CUP, 1997

Foley, H., 'The Conception of Women in Athenian Drama' in H. Foley (ed.), *Reflections of Women in Antiquity*, New York, Gordon and Breach, 1981

Goldhill, Simon, *Reading Greek Tragedy*, Cambridge, CUP, 1986

Green, J. R., *Theatre in Ancient Greek Society*, London, Routledge, 1994

Green, J. R. and Handley E., *Images of the Greek Theatre*, London, British Museum Press, 1995

Jones, J., *On Aristotle and Greek Tragedy*, London, Chatto and Windus, 1962

Knox, Bernard (ed.), *Word and Action: Essays on the Ancient Theatre*, Baltimore, Johns Hopkins University Press, 1979

Ley, G., *A Short Introduction to the Greek Theatre*, Chicago, University of Chicago Press, 1991

Pickard-Cambridge, A., *The Dramatic Festivals of Athens*, 2nd ed. revised J. Gould and D. M. Lewis, Oxford, OUP, 1968

Rehm, Rush, *Greek Tragic Theatre*, London, Routledge, 1992

Taplin, Oliver, *Greek Tragedy in Action*, London, Methuen, 1978

——, *The Stagecraft of Aeschylus: The Dramatic Use of Exits and Entrances in Greek Tragedy*, Oxford, Clarendon Press, 1977

Walcot, Peter, *Greek Drama in its Theatrical and Social Context*, Cardiff, University of Wales Press, 1976

Walton, J. Michael, *Greek Theatre Practice*, London, Methuen, 1980

——, *The Greek Sense of Theatre*, London, Methuen, 1984

——, *Living Greek Theatre: A Handbook of Classical Performance and Modern Production*, Westport, Greenwood Press, 1988

Wiles, David, *Tragedy in Athens*, Cambridge, CUP, 1997

——, *Greek Theatre Performance: An Introduction*, Cambridge, CUP, 2000

Winkler, J. J. and Zeitlin, F. I. (eds), *Nothing To Do With Dionysos – Athenian Drama in its Social Context*, Princeton, Princeton University Press, 1990

Zimmermann, B., *Greek Tragedy: An Introduction*, trans., Marier, Baltimore, Johns Hopkins University Press, 1990

General studies of Sophocles

Bloom, H., *Sophocles*, Philadelphia, Chelsea House, 1990
Blundell, M. W., *Helping Friends and Harming Enemies: A Study in Sophocles and Greek Ethics*, Cambridge, CUP, 1989
Burton, R. W. B., *The Chorus in Sophocles' Tragedies*, Oxford, OUP, 1980
Buxton, R. G., *Sophocles*, Oxford, OUP, 1984
Gardiner, C. P., *The Sophoclean Chorus,* Iowa City, University of Iowa Press, 1987
Gellie, G. H., *Sophocles*, Melbourne, Melbourne University Press, 1972
Kirkwood, G. M., *A Study of Sophoclean Drama*, Ithaca, Cornell University Press, 1958; 2nd ed. 1994
Kitto, H. D. F., *Sophocles: Dramatist and Philosopher,* London, Greenwood Press, 1958
Knox, B. M. W., *The Heroic Temper*, Berkeley and Los Angeles, University of California Press, 1964
Seale, D., *Vision and Stagecraft in Sophocles*, London, Croom Helm, 1982
Segal, C. P., *Sophocles' Tragic World: Divinity, Nature, Society*, Cambridge MA, Harvard University Press, 1995
——, *Tragedy and Civilization: An Interpretation of Sophocles,* Cambridge, CUP, 1981
Waldock, A. J. A., *Sophocles the Dramatist*, Cambridge, CUP, 1951
Webster, T. B. L., *An Introduction to Sophocles*, 2nd ed., London, Methuen, 1969
Whitman, C. H., *Sophocles: A Study of Heroic Humanism,* Cambridge MA, Harvard University Press, 1951
Winnington-Ingram, R. P., *Sophocles*, Cambridge, CUP, 1980
Woodard, T. (ed.), *Sophocles: A Collection of Critical Essays,* Englewood Cliffs, NJ, Prentice Hall, 1966

Studies and articles on *Oedipus the King*

Ahl, F., *Sophocles' 'Oedipus': Evidence and Self-Conviction,* Ithaca, Cornell University Press, 1991
Bloom, H. (ed.), *Modern Critical Interpretations, Sophocles: 'Oedipus Rex'*, Philadelphia, Chelsea House, 1988
Bushnell, Rebecca, W., *Prophesying Tragedy: Sign and Voice in*

Sophocles' 'Theban Plays', Ithaca, Cornell University Press, 1988

Burton, R. W. B., *The Chorus in Sophocles' Tragedies*, Oxford, OUP, 1980

Cameron, A., *The Identity of Oedipus the King: Five Essays on the 'Oedipus Tyrannus'*, NY, New York University Press, 1968

Champlin, M. W., '*Oedipus Tyrannus* and the Problem of Knowledge', *Classical Journal*, lxiv, 1969, pp. 337–45

Dodds, E. R., 'On Misunderstanding the *Oedipus Rex*' in *The Ancient Concept of Progress,* Oxford, OUP, 1973, pp. 64–77

Edmunds, L., *Oedipus: The Ancient Legend and its Later Analogues*, Baltimore, Johns Hopkins University Press, 1985

——, *Oedipus*, London and New York, Routledge, 2006

Freud, Sigmund, '*Oedipus Rex*' in *Sophocles: A Collection of Critical Essays*, ed. T. Woodard, Englewood Cliffs, NJ, Prentice Hall, 1966

Gardiner, C. P., *The Sophoclean Chorus: A Study of Character and Function*, Iowa, University of Iowa Press, 1987

Griffith, R. D., *The Theatre of Apollo: Divine Justice and 'Oedipus the King',* Montreal, McGill/Queens Press, 1996

Knox, B. M. W., *Oedipus at Thebes*, New Haven and London, Yale University Press, 1957

——, 'Why is Oedipus called Tyrannos?', *Classical Journal,* 50, 1954, pp. 97–102

Pucci, P., 'Oedipus and the Fabrication of the Father: *Oedipus Tyrannus*' in *Modern Criticism and Philosophy*, Baltimore, Johns Hopkins University Press, 1992

——, 'The Tragic *Pharmakos* of the *Oedipus Rex*', *Helios*, xvii, 1990, pp. 41–9

Segal, C., 'Time and Knowledge in the Tragedy of Oedipus' in *Sophocles' Tragic World: Divinity, Nature, Society,* Cambridge MA, Harvard University Press, 1995

Stanford, W. B., 'Ambiguities in the *Oedipus Tyrannus*' in *Ambiguity in Greek Literature,* Oxford, OUP, 1939, pp. 163–73

Vellacott, P., *Sophocles and Oedipus: A Study of 'Oedipus Tyrannus' with a New Translation,* London, Macmillan, 1971

Vernant, J. P., 'Ambiguity and Reversal: On the Enigmatic Structure of *Oedipus Rex*' in J. P. Vernant and P. Vidal-Noquet (eds), *Myth and Tragedy in Ancient Greece*, trans. Janet Lloyd, New York, Zone Books, 1988, pp. 113–40

Modern reception of *Oedipus the King*

Burian, P., 'Tragedy Adapted for Stages and Screens: The Renaissance to the Present' in P. E. Easterling (ed.), *The Cambridge Companion to Greek Tragedy*, Cambridge, CUP, 1997, pp. 228–83

Hall, E., Macintosh, F., and Wrigley, A. (eds), *Dionysus since '69: Tragedy at the Dawn of the Millennium*, Oxford, OUP, 2004

Macintosh, F., 'Tragedy in Performance: Nineteenth- and Twentieth-century Productions' in P. E. Easterling (ed.), *The Cambridge Companion to Greek Tragedy*, Cambridge, CUP, 1997, pp. 284–323

O'Brien, M. J. (ed.), *Twentieth-Century Interpretations of 'Oedipus Rex'*, Englewood Cliffs, Prentice Hall, 1968

Websites

http://duke.usask.ca/porterj/skenotheke.html: 'Skenotheke: Images of the Ancient Stage' provides valuable visual evidence of stagecraft in classical times

www.apgrd.ox.ac.uk: 'The Archive of Performances of Greek and Roman Drama' contains useful information on the reception of Greek drama in modern performances (reviews of productions, books, current research, events)

http://www2.open.ac.uk/ClassicalStudies/GreekPlays/index.html: also useful on the reception of Greek drama

http:/www.didaskalia.net/index.html: electronic journal on Greek and Roman theatre

http://depthome.brooklyn.cuny.edu/classics/dunkle/tragedy/index.htm: general introduction to Greek tragedy

http://www.theatron.co.uk/: a virtual reality tool for teaching and researching theatre history

Translator's Note

Sophocles English'd

'Bless thee, Bottom, bless thee, thou art translated,' cries the literary-minded Peter Quince, when he sees his noisy amateur actor friend's earnest bonce metamorphosed into a braying ass-head – and Shakespeare's pun is exact: translation – particularly the translation of poetry – involves a fundamental metamorphosis of form. A poem may be written in blank verse, rhyme royal or *terza rima,* but even closer to the heart of the matter is the language it is written in. The words themselves are the underlying form of a poem, because it is only in the actual and precise choice of words that meaning and association, and feeling and music and shape, and all the other elements that go to make up a poem – reside. That is why genuine translation, the lateral movement of something called a poem from one language across to another, is impossible. It can only be transformed, re-shaped in a quite new formal structure, ass-head instead of man-head: and then, if it is any good, it becomes pure ass, essentially asinine, with only the memory of the man remaining. A good poem translated, must become a good poem in its new language, not merely a memory of the old. When Brecht was up before the un-American activities committee, a committee-man solemnly read out a translation of one of Brecht's poems, as evidence of his Communist connections. 'Mr Brecht,' accused the committee-man, 'did you write this poem?' 'No,' replied Brecht, 'I wrote a very similar poem, in German.'

In fact, it is this dilemma that makes the impossible art of translation so endlessly rewarding. If it were simply a matter of transferring blocks of meaning from one language to another, we would programme our computers, and leave them to get on with it. But good translations, because they must live in their new linguistic surroundings, express as much of the translator as of the translated. We read Pope's Homer and Dryden's Virgil for Pope and Dryden, not Homer and Virgil: and who could deny that Tony Harrison's *Oresteia,* controversial as it is in its individuality, is as much a part of Tony Harrison's struggle to bring the northern voice into its own in modern English poetry, as it is a version of Aeschylus?

The truth of the matter is that translations serve as many different purposes as there are translators, and at least four major kinds can be identified. The first is the literal translation, or crib, staff and companion of generations of students, good old indispensable Loeb. These are usually written in an execrable alien English, never spoken or even written anywhere else by the inhabitants of this planet, and full of words like 'suppliant', 'filet' and 'hecatombs', precise enough renderings of Greek and Roman realities, but utterly incomprehensible as lived English.

The second kind is the most ambitious, and the most common: the attempt to render as much of the poem as possible in the new language, trying to reproduce meaning, verse form, style, and even the musical movement of the original. This was attempted on an heroic scale by Dorothy L. Sayers' version of *The Divine Comedy,* but it can easily collapse into a twisted unidiomatic mish-mash, a game for contortionists, tying an elegant human shape into ugly knots in the pursuit of the impossible.

In the third kind of translation, the translator allows himself a considerable amount of freedom, to express the spirit rather than the letter of the original text. His main concern is to recreate the feel and impact of the original as completely as he can, and he allows himself the freedom to travel quite far from the original writer's literal meaning and style: but his overall intention remains to get as close to that original writer as he can, and he still sees himself as servant rather than master. Pope and Dryden might reasonably be described as translators of this kind, and Ezra Pound's aggressively slangy version of *The Women of Trachis* joins that company in kind if not achievement.

The fourth kind, imitation, or re-composition, is effectively the creation of a new work, based on or inspired by an original text in another language, and it is here perhaps that the finest poetry is to be found – many hundreds of Elizabethan love sonnets, Johnson's *London* and *The Vanity of Human Wishes,* imitated from Juvenal, Pope's *Imitation of Horace,* and more recently, Robert Lowell's *Imitations.* We can't go to such poems for anything resembling a version of the original text, more often a perceptive commentary on the nature of the two cultures and ages compared: in Johnson's case, with the insight of genius.

Where does my own translation of the Theban Plays stand? The answer is not quite in any of the four sections, though perhaps nearer to the third than any other. What differentiates it from that third section, creating, in effect, a sub-section of its own, is that I have no Greek, and have worked from one specially commissioned literal translation, and a consideration of the work of many of my distinguished predecessors.

Of course, I did not sit down one bright morning and say to myself, 'I don't read a word of classical Greek, I'll translate Sophocles.' Wearing my other hat as a director, I was discussing with the BBC producer Louis Marks, the possibility of presenting some Greek tragedy on television. My main interest at that time was in setting up a production of Euripides' *The Trojan Women*. It hadn't occurred to me to suggest a trilogy of plays, because as a freelance I knew it was unlikely that I would succeed in getting even one Greek play onto television, let alone three. A few days later, Louis Marks rang me with the totally unexpected suggestion that we should tackle the whole *Theban Trilogy*, and my first reaction was somewhere between awe, delight and disbelief: but I soon grasped the point he had perceived, that there would probably be a greater chance of selling a project on this grand scale to the decision-makers in the BBC than there would be of selling them what in television parlance we would call a one-off Greek play. Louis Marks' instinct proved right. Though we were originally given the go-ahead only for *Antigone* – which had an effect on the translation – Louis' careful political instinct managed eventually, over a period of more than two years, to guide the Sophoclean trireme through the dangerous waters of BBC politics, and bring her safely to port.

We then considered what translation to use, and immediately we were confronted with a huge problem, crucial to the success of the whole project. We were both determined to present these wonderful plays, one of the cornerstones of European culture, in such a way as to reveal at least something of their stature, and why they have been considered the yardstick by which drama is measured for 2,500 years. In television, we were both well aware, the problem is enormously magnified by the fact that the vast majority of our audience would know nothing at all of classical Greek drama, and those who did know something of it would probably be prejudiced by the vulgar notion that it is gloomy, boring and out of date. We were quite determined not to talk down or sell Sophocles short. Our productions would have to be convincing and a pleasure to Greek scholars who have spent a life studying the texts, and a thrillingly compelling new world opening up for viewers to whom Attic tragedy wasn't even a name.

Though television is a good medium for genuine dramatic poetry, it is merciless with any kind of stilted language, and it soon became clear to us that we could present none of the existing translations of the Sophoclean trilogy with the faintest chance of the particular kind of success we hoped for.

At this point, I decided that I ought to do the job myself. The playwright-translator without the original language is a not uncommon figure now, and in poetic drama, where the quality of the language is of the greatest importance, he has even more justification for his existence than in more naturalistic forms. The idea had already been mooted in our earliest discussions about *The Trojan Women.* At that time I had had sixteen of my own original TV plays presented, as well as nine stage plays in theatres around the country, and I had already written and directed the first TV play to be written in verse, *The Testament of John,* though it had not yet been transmitted. Louis Marks had himself been the producer on several of these plays, including *The Testament of John,* and he was very happy to agree with the idea. We discovered, to our amazement, that as far as our researches could probe, the whole *Theban Trilogy* had never been translated complete by a working playwright. It had been left to Greek scholars and poets to do the job. But these great works were written for public performance in a well-established and highly competitive theatre, by men who were themselves poets, singers, actors, composers and dancers, as well as directors of their own plays. That fact convinced me. It was surely time for a playwright to get a look in, even if he did have no Greek.

Before I set a word on paper, I bumped into my friend the actor Patrick Stewart. I mentioned that I was just about to begin translating Sophocles, and I was very surprised when he made a wry face and said he didn't much like Greek tragedy. I was astounded at this in so distinguished an actor, and one, too, so eminently well suited to Greek roles, and I said so. He replied that he had been in many productions, but had always found that the plays were difficult to act well because the actor found himself again and again involved in tremendous dramatic situations which were expressed in the most banal language, and that he himself could never find a satisfactory way of marrying the power of the situations to the poverty of the words. No more useful comment could have been made to me as I began the huge project. I determined that whatever else I did, and however much of a limitation my lack of knowledge of the Sophoclean original was bound to be, I would at least make sure I gave the actors some decent English words to say.

About one thing I was quite clear from the beginning: that these plays are non-naturalistic poetic drama, at the very highest level of the art, certainly the equal of Shakespeare, and that the poverty-stricken speech of modern naturalism, particularly the film-based television variety, would have no place in my versions. That I would write in verse was not a matter of choice, but the point I started from.

When I wrote *The Testament of John,* I had already confronted the problem that faces every twentieth-century English writer attempting drama in verse, namely, what verse form to use. I was quite convinced that the standard iambic pentameter is no longer a possibility in drama. Shakespeare, Milton, Wordsworth and Keats have done all there is to be done with that particular music: for me, at least, their shadow is far too large. So I looked back at the last successful attempt to write verse drama in English, and saw T. S. Eliot. I find his drama very unsympathetic, nor do I see in it any evidence that he possessed those particular qualities which make a writer a playwright. He seems to me to be a part of that long tradition in English letters of major poets who were fascinated by the drama without having any aptitude for it, and the plays he wrote and had successfully performed, a triumph of sheer intellect, a great poet's attempt to do something for which he was fundamentally unsuited. But nevertheless, he had been the first poet-playwright to confront the problem of a suitable verse form for modern drama; he too had rejected the iambic pentameter, and whatever the limitations of his plays as plays, he had created many passages of fine dramatic verse: so I decided to try to use his form to serve my own purposes.

Eliot had created a verse line, loosely based on Anglo-Saxon poetry, but without the alliteration, a line consisting of four feet, in which each foot had to contain one strong beat, but could contain any number of weak ones. In doing so he created a verse movement close to the rhythms of natural speech, with something of the flexibility of prose, but which, with the regular beat of its four stresses, clearly defined a recognisable verse music. The problem this metre sets a writer, one which I have not overcome, is that many lines remain ambiguous in stress, clear enough in the poet's mind perhaps, but capable of more than one kind of scansion. In spite of my strictures, the reader will find plenty of iambic pentameters in the five thousand-odd lines of verse in this book. But the experience of directing these translations suggests to me that the problem is an abstract one, more apparent than real. In the mouths of actors, it tends to disappear. The skill involved, as in all dramatic verse, is for the playwright's instinct for natural stress in dramatic English to coincide naturally and without strain with the formal pattern of the verse: and the freer that pattern, the finer the poet's ear must be. This was the metre I had attempted with *The Testament of John,* so it was natural that I should use it for the dramatic trimeters of Sophoclean tragedy. I decided not to be absolutely strict with myself, and to allow the occasional two- or three-footed line if I wanted it. But I tried to make sure that I only used the shorter line for positive effect, not simply because I couldn't think of any way of filling up the odd feet!

The lyric verse in these plays confronts the translator with his biggest problem, but here my experience as a theatrical practitioner helped me. As a director, I had already decided how I intended to present the choral odes. They had to create a quite new lyrical dramatic experience, utterly differentiated from the dramatic episodes. So Sophocles' formal odes would not be broken up, shared out between the chorus actors and spoken as individual lines, to make them seem as naturalistic as possible. I would use a chorus of twelve (Sophocles himself increased the number of the chorus from twelve to fifteen, but I decided upon twelve because it is divisible by six, four, three, two and one, and would therefore make more interesting formal groupings) and the characters would speak to the accompaniment of live specially composed music, in unison, as individuals, and in all the possible sub-groupings. My lyric verse had to be English lyric verse, with its own life and vitality, so this meant that my models had to be not the Greek originals, whose texture was beyond my comprehension anyway, but the masters of English lyric verse, Keats, Shelley, Marvell, Donne, Jonson, the Cavalier poets, the young Milton. I would try to write tightly rhyming verses, using metres and verse movements imitated from these masters, and I would strive most of all to make these odes convincing as dramatic lyrics in their own right. Where Sophocles in a chorus or choral dialogue repeated the metrical form of a strophe with an exactly similar antistrophe, so I would repeat my lyric verses with meticulous accuracy, strictly reflecting metrical form and rhyme scheme. I would be particularly careful to avoid the use of thunderous full rhymes all the time, using half-rhyme, and even quarter-rhyme – the matching of final consonants only – to ensure flexibility and avoid musical banality. This was not an original decision, I knew. Many translators have tried to rhyme their choruses, using these or similar techniques. But I knew of none that had attempted it with the thoroughgoing concern for form that I intended: nor, indeed, any that were really good enough as English lyric verse. Yeats, of course, made famous versions of choruses from *Antigone* and *Oedipus at Colonus,* but they are a long way from Sophocles, Yeatsian poems in their own right, based on Sophoclean ideas, rather than usable translations.

But that strategic decision left a whole series of tactical questions unanswered. Lyric metres are used in Greek tragedy in a whole series of different ways, in the entry song of the chorus (*parados*) in the choral odes (*stasima*), the choral dialogues (*kommoi*), in the *exodos,* which often takes the form of a choral dialogue, and even, in moments of excitement, within the dramatic episodes themselves. As a point of principle, I decided that whenever Sophocles used lyric verse, I would use my English lyric form, but I very soon discovered that this decision had considerable implications. Most of the greatest moments – one might almost say all of them – in these three plays are written by Sophocles in the form of choral dialogues, an interaction, in lyric verse, between the chorus and one or two of the main characters. Oedipus' re-entry blinded, his recital of his woes at Colonus, Antigone's farewell to the chorus, Antigone's and Ismene's threnody for the dead Oedipus, and Creon's dirge over his dead son and wife, are all cast by Sophocles in the form of *kommoi*, or formal choral dialogues, often with the most sophisticated poetic skill, in the exact repetition of metrical patterns from verse to verse, and in the breaking up of single lines between several voices. But these sections are usually translated either into prose, or into a loose free verse, with scarcely any differentiation made between them and the normal dramatic episodes. It immediately became clear that these sections represent the moments of the most intense grief and sorrow in the plays, and it is here that the poet has chosen to stylise his work most completely, to remove it utterly from the prosaic world of daily speech – which had little enough part in the world of Greek tragedy anyway – into the world of music, poetry and dance, a world in which grief can be expressed in its purest, most essential form. The wrong kind of naturalism is the greatest danger for twentieth-century actors and directors when attempting the Greeks. That kind of thinking would require Oedipus simply to mutter 'Christ, my eyes hurt' and fall down the steps when he enters blinded. The very fact that he does not say that, but utters a lyric poem, to music, is the essence of the kind of play we are dealing with. Here, too, was the answer to the subversive question that Patrick Stewart had planted in my mind. A tremendous situation requires tremendous things to be said, requires a poem of despair or suffering, upon which the actor can launch himself, and take wing. So the choral dialogues too would have to be written in tightly rhyming lyric verse, and acted to music. The further I looked into this, the more interesting the idea became. It is not only moments of grief and sorrow that Sophocles renders in his *kommoi*, but moments of high drama, like the climax of the row between Oedipus, Creon and Jocasta in *Oedipus the King*, and Creon's seizure of Oedipus in *Oedipus at Colonus*. These, too, most modern translations render in an informal, 'naturalistic' way, and these too I decided to translate into lyric verse, and act to music.

This decision had further implications. I had never intended to attempt to reproduce anything of Sophocles' own verse movement, music or texture – indeed, as a non-Greek reader, it was impossible that I should. But the decision to render such a large part of the plays into lyric verse meant that the translation must necessarily become freer. In the irreconcilable conflict between a literal rendering of all the subtleties of Sophocles' original, and the severe demands of English rhyming lyric verse, the needs of the latter would have to come first, if I was to avoid desperate convolutions and unidiomatic phraseology. My version of the choral odes and dialogues, if it was to do any sort of justice to Sophocles' drama by creating passages of striking, and emotionally moving English, might have to do less than justice to his words. In practice this has meant the occasional use of metaphors not in the original, and the pursuit of ideas or the completion of concepts which Sophocles has not pursued or completed. Simply, there were times when I let my pen have its way, to complete the poem as my instinct told me it had to be completed, and the reader must be left to judge to what degree this is acceptable. Transformation is required, not transliteration. We need a new English poem, full of its own energy and vitality, not a pale reflection of the old.

*

Style was an equally crucial consideration, though here it was easier to see the road that had to be followed. We had decided on a new translation in the first place because we couldn't find one that was written in direct, modern theatrical English, the language employed by the best practitioners on the modern stage. We wanted no archaisms, no inversions, no puffing up of the emotions by Victorian rhodomontade. The great moments had to be earned, through a simple, strong, concrete, metaphorical English, with no vulgar indulgence of modernity or affectation of the ancient. The ambition was to make the language and the ideas expressed within it, as simple, direct and powerful as it must have been to its original spectators, and if this meant a simplification of mythological nomenclature, and the insertion of a few words or lines to make clear an idea that has not survived the journey of 2,500 years, so be it. Two simple examples will suffice. The Greek gods are invoked by many different names, expressing different elements of the same deity, but I have tended to use only one. Apollo remains Apollo, not Phoebus, the Delian, the Archer King, Loxias, or whatever. More importantly, in *Antigone,* all the original spectators would have known the horrific significance of a body remaining unburied – namely, that there was no chance of peace in the underworld until the correct rites had been performed. Creon is damning Polynices' eternal soul, as Hamlet or Isabella might have put it, as well as his body. Sophocles nowhere says this, because all his audience knew it, but I have inserted a line or two in the earlier part of the play to make the tragic issue quite clear.

The actual usage of words is always the most personal matter in any writer's style, and in this way my own verbal personality must be reflected in every line of the play. One of the clearest indications of this is perhaps in the use of certain modern words which in the purest sense would be considered anachronisms. Rumour, in *Colonus*, travels 'faster than an Olympic champion', and Eurydice in *Antigone* remarks that 'We are bred to stoicism in this family'. Zeno of Citium began to develop stoic philosophy a clear four generations after Sophocles' lifetime, and the Olympic Games began in the eighth century BC, many hundreds of years after the Heroic age. But the word 'stoicism' in modern English has nothing at all to do with the philosophy of Zeno. The word has become a part of general modern usage, representing endurance of an intense and uncomplaining kind; just as the phrase 'Olympic champion' doesn't represent to us anything specifically Greek, nor even a specific modern champion, an Ovett or Coe, but the idea of world supremacy in sport: in this particular case, the fastest. People who object to such usages will probably also object to words like 'realpolitik', 'security police', and Antigone's description of Hades as 'that bleak hotel which is never short of a room': but I stand by my usages. In performance they work well, expressing in a vivid modern way an idea that does not seem un-Sophoclean. They are I suppose the standard-bearers or forlorn hope of my attack on the problem of style. My loyalty, as a translator of a text written for performance, must always be principally to the language being translated into, not the language being translated from. That is where my attempt will succeed or fail, not in the details of my treatment, or maltreatment, of the original.

One external factor had an effect on these translations. I was originally commissioned to translate all three plays, and I worked on them in story order, beginning with page one of *Oedipus the King*. Most of the problems of form and style were confronted within the process of translating the first play, but obviously I learned as I went along. I didn't feel that I had really learned how to translate the formal odes and choral dialogues until I was about halfway through *Colonus,* and when I looked back on the completed first draft, it seemed to me that *Antigone* was, by a long way, the best of the three, as by that time I was confident in what I was doing. In these first drafts, I had made no attempt to reproduce exactly the formal patterns of the choruses and choral dialogues. I had allowed my own verse forms to emerge naturally, and simply repeated them where repetition was required. The passages of stichomythia likewise, I kept as sharp as I could, but did not attempt to reproduce the formal one line or two line patterns of the original. My translations came out quite a lot longer than the originals, of course, but I had expected that. Part of the greatness of any poet lies in his compression of language, and I knew that that was one of many areas where I couldn't hope to be in Sophocles' league.

It was decided to produce *Antigone* first. In the light of advice from Geoffrey Lewis, my classical mentor, I made several crucial retranslations, but *Antigone* went into production much as originally drafted. A year passed before the next two plays were scheduled for production, and during that time I did a great deal of revision and retranslation. I had always been dissatisfied with the first half of *Oedipus the King*, and while reworking it, I found that I was in fact capable of making versions of Sophocles' odes which were much closer to Sophocles' own length, and I soon discovered the delights of reproducing the stichomythia patterns exactly. When I moved onto *Oedipus at Colonus*, I was very conscious that I was courting disaster by letting the English play become too long. The original Greek text is the longest in the canon, and my first version sprawled to some two-and-a-half hours playing-time. So I took a deep breath and decided to attempt to do all the choruses, choral dialogues, and stichomythic passages in the same numbers and patterns of lines employed in the original Greek, which, although I could not read it, was always at my elbow, so that its formal patterns, or those of them that can be clearly seen on the page, were clear to me. My versions are still longer, of course, even when I employ exactly the same number of lines as the original Greek: but they are not so much longer as to threaten the plays' structure, and the formal patterns, in *Colonus* at least, are absolutely reproduced. In this formal respect, *Colonus* is the closest of the translations. *Oedipus the King* is almost as close, and *Antigone* is the freest of the three. [. . .]

'A poem,' as Auden said, 'is never finished. You simply stop working on it.' The needs of production gave me an unavoidable deadline, but all three plays have been allowed the luxury of some degree of retranslation after the productions. In the first two plays only the odd line or phrase has been changed, but in *Antigone,* the degree of reworking has been considerable.

Sophocles is one of us, not one of a lost them, buried in centuries of dust in forgotten libraries. He is alive now, he lives in our world, and because he is alive, his ideas have changed subtly over the centuries, as mankind has acquired more experience against which to measure his work. Because he was one of the greatest of theatrical artists his work stands up to this scrutiny of the succeeding generations, and as we bring to it our own experience, it becomes richer and more revealing. So there must be nothing archaeological about the act of translation, nothing of the creation of vanished historical epochs. We owe him the best, most idiomatic, up-to-date language we can manage, so that the burning immediacy and power of his art can strike us as powerfully as they struck his contemporaries. My main aim in making this new version of these much-translated works has been to make them seem that they were written not 2,500 years ago, but the day before yesterday, today, and tomorrow.

OEDIPUS THE KING

CHARACTERS

OEDIPUS, King of Thebes
A PRIEST of Zeus
CREON, brother of Jocasta
TEIRESIAS, a prophet, blind
JOCASTA, wife of Oedipus
CORINTHIAN MESSENGER
OLD SHEPHERD
MESSENGER
CHORUS of Counsellors of Thebes
TEIRESIAS' BOY
ANTIGONE } daughters of Oedipus and Jocasta
ISMENE }
PEOPLE OF THEBES
JOCASTA'S WOMEN
SHEPHERD'S ATTENDANTS

This translation was commissioned by BBC Television and first produced in the autumn of 1986, with the following cast:

OEDIPUS	Michael Pennington
CREON	John Shrapnel
TEIRESIAS	John Gielgud
JOCASTA	Claire Bloom
SHEPHERD	David Waller
MESSENGER	Gerard Murphy
PRIEST	Cyril Cusack
CORINTHIAN MESSENGER	Norman Rodway
ANTIGONE	Cassie Shilling
ISMENE	Kelly Huntley
TEIRESIAS' BOY	Lincoln Saunders
CHORUS	Nigel Stock, Edward Hardwicke, Donald Eccles, Robert Eddison, Alan Rowe, Denys Hawthorne, David Collings, Michael Byrne, Noel Johnson, Ernest Clark, Clifford Rose, John Woodnutt
PEOPLE OF THEBES	Gabrielle Blunt, Imogen Claire, Edwina Day, Mary Lincoln, Heather Ramsay, Judy Liebert, Catherine Shipton, Mary Llewellen, Czeslaw Grocholski, Stuart Saunders, Bill Gavin, Gordon Faith, Philip Wright, Alan Collins, Richard Tate, Timothy Block, Stanley Dawson, Michael Eaves, Hugh Hayes, Eric Longworth, Judith Cox, Anne Higgins, Hazel Stock, Susie Sapsford, Elizabeth Page, Gioia Izquierdo, Jacqui Cryer, Mike Vinden, Colin Thomas, Kenneth Lawrie, John Coleman, Andrew Thompson, Bernard Losh
CHILDREN OF THEBES	Tamsin Alker, Erica Rossi, Nicola Whitehead, Dean Gunter, Nicola Sideris, Emma Cook, Tom Hammond, Lincoln Saunders, Jonathan Taylor, Lucy Hammond

Directed by	Don Taylor
Produced by	Louis Marks
Designed by	David Myerscough-Jones
Music by	Derek Bourgeois
Costumes by	June Hudson

The scene is set before the palace of King Oedipus in the city of Thebes.

Citizens of Thebes, of all ages, enter, or are discovered. They carry with them garlanded laurel branches and incense burners, and they show all the signs of the sickness which is ravaging the city.

Led by a PRIEST *of Zeus, they gather in groups in front of the king's palace, adopting attitudes of desperation and prayer.*

The palace doors open.

Enter OEDIPUS.

OEDIPUS. My children. You are the modern descendants
Of King Cadmus, who founded our city.
Why do you come here with these laurel branches,
Ritually dressed, and all the signs
Of desperate people begging for help?
In the city I hear prayers for the sick,
And the sound of weeping. The air is heavy
With incense and tears. What more do you want?
I can't rely on second-hand reports,
I have come to find out for myself.
I am Oedipus the king. Everyone knows my name.
You, sir, you are a priest,
A man old enough to be wise
And entitled to speak first. A sudden panic
Is it, or a demand for action?
Anything I can do, I will do, of course.
I would have to be a man without feeling
To close my eyes and stop my ears
To a petition from everyone, such as this.

PRIEST. King Oedipus, Lord of Thebes,
You see us, many hundreds crowding to your palace:
Youngsters, like birds still in the nest,
Old men, whose eyes have seen everything,
Priests – of Zeus, like me – and of other gods,
And the very best of our young men.
We have all come here: there are thousands more
Sitting in the market place, carrying emblems like these,
Others at the two altars of Pallas Athene,
And at Ismenus' shrine by the river bank
Where the future can be read in the ashes,
And we are all offering desperate prayers.

You've seen yourself what's happening here.
This city is like a warship, defeated in battle
Wallowing aimlessly in a sea of blood.
The crops are rotting in the fields,
Disease is killing all the cattle,
Babies are born dead, or decay in the womb,
And as if that weren't enough, some god has sent plague
Like a fire-demon to scorch our people.
The courtyards Cadmus built will soon be empty,
And the underworld is already crowded with Thebans
Weeping in the darkness for themselves and their kin.
If we choose to come here to beg for help,
It's not because we think of you as a god,
But because we know you to be the best of men,
Not only in the daily business of the state,
But in those deeper mysteries of life
Where the mind of man touches eternity.
We haven't forgotten that it was you,
A young man, newly arrived here,
Who solved the riddle of the Sphinx,
That monstrous perversion of woman, lion and bird,
And freed us from her magical tyranny.
We could do nothing to help you then,
And I think – we all think – some god helped you.
That's why, world-famous Oedipus,
We're asking for your help again. Find us
Some remedy, either from your own experience,
Or by calling on supernatural powers.
You've solved terrible problems in the past,
And that gives us confidence in your abilities now
Indeed, you have a reputation to live up to.
Your genius has saved us once. It would be
Ridiculous to have preserved us then,
Only to see us wasted now.
Save us again, as you did before.
Sail under that same lucky star,
And guide us, as a real prince should,
Into the harbour of good fortune and peace.
An unmanned ship needs no captain:
A city that is empty because its people are dead
Has no further use for a king.

OEDIPUS. My children, believe me when I say
I know everything that you are suffering,
Why you come here, and what you ask of me.
I suffer as much, perhaps more than you do.
You carry your personal burdens of sorrow:
I carry them too, and my own, and the city's.
I have not been sleeping. My eyes, like yours,
Are bloodshot with too frequent tears.
I have walkèd every corridor of the palace,
And all the secret galleries of my mind,
Searching and searching what best to do.
And this much I have done – because I haven't been idle –
The one thing that seemed sensible.
My brother-in-law, Creon, the son of Menoeceus,
I have sent to the oracle of Apollo, at Delphi,
To ask the Pythia, the sacred priestess,
What action or word of mine might help.
He ought to be here, his mission has taken
Far longer than it should, and I begin to wonder
What keeps him so long. When he arrives,
Whatever the oracle demands, you have my word
Will be meticulously performed.
PRIEST. No man could say better than that;
Nor upon a better cue. Look, there's the signal!
Creon himself is approaching.
OEDIPUS. Whatever the message, he's certainly smiling!
Apollo, god of healing, let the news be good.
PRIEST. It must be good. He moves like a man.
Confident of his success.
OEDIPUS. He can hear us now.
Dear brother-in-law! Son of Menoeceus!
Enter CREON.
What's the god's message? What does the oracle say?
CREON. It's good news. Or perhaps I should say
It will be good news, if all turns out well:
Though perhaps painful to begin with.
OEDIPUS. And what does that mean! At such an answer
I don't know if I should laugh or cry!
CREON. Do you want me to say it all here, in public,
Or shall we go in?
OEDIPUS. In public, of course!

While these people suffer, I suffer too.
Their life concerns me, more than my own!
CREON. The answer is straightforward, and the command simple.
There is something unclean in our city.
Born here. Living here. It pollutes everything.
We harbour it. We must drive it out.
OEDIPUS. How can it be purified, the pollution of
This unclean thing? What is it?
CREON. By banishment. Or by blood for blood.
It was bloodshed, the oracle says,
That whipped up this storm that's destroying us.
OEDIPUS. Whose blood was shed? What sort of man?
CREON. There was a king here sir, before you came.
His name was Laius.
OEDIPUS. I know the name.
I never saw the man.
CREON. The man was killed:
And the oracle's meaning is clear enough.
The murderers of Laius must be found,
And the unknown killers brought to justice.
OEDIPUS. But where are they? The trail's gone cold.
It's an old story now. Where shall we begin?
CREON. Here. The god said here. Search,
And you won't be disappointed. No evidence
Is ever found if you don't look for it.
OEDIPUS. Where did it happen – this unexplained murder?
Was it here in the palace? Or in the country?
Or while he was travelling abroad?
CREON. He left the city to make a pilgrimage.
And he never came back, except in a coffin.
OEDIPUS. Who was with him? Didn't anyone see it?
There must be evidence, some scrap, some rumour?
CREON. One of the servants escaped. He ran
So fast, he could only remember one thing.
OEDIPUS. What thing? Tell me. The smallest clue
Might lead to others.
CREON. He said that robbers,
Not one man, a whole band of them,
Met them on the road and they murdered the king.
OEDIPUS. Robbers? Would they dare attack a king?
Perhaps they were bought. Theban money,

And political ambition the motive.
CREON. We thought that too, at first. But the crisis
Blew up almost at once. We had other troubles,
And Laius was dead. No one pursued it.
OEDIPUS. What crisis could be greater than a murdered king?
So there never was a full investigation?
CREON. The voice of the Sphinx seemed to mesmerise us.
She drained all our energies with her riddling.
It was a question of survival: no time
For unsolved mysteries, even regicide.
OEDIPUS. Then I shall begin it. There's time enough now.
We'll shine a fresh light into every corner
Of the whole dark and musty business.
Thanks to the Lord Apollo! And our gratitude to you,
Creon, for reminding us what we had forgotten,
Our duty to the dead. I am determined
To do everything I can to help our city
And show the god's justice. It's in my interest too
To avenge this crime, not only for Laius' sake,
But for my own protection. This unknown killer
Might strike at me. Justice for Laius
And my own safety go hand in hand.
So go to your homes, dear people, my children,
Pick up your sad sprays of laurel
Call the Theban counsellors here, and tell them
That I will do everything man can do.
With the god's help, we will find out the truth
And save the city. We must, or be destroyed.
Exit OEDIPUS, *into the palace.*
PRIEST. Go home, now, good people. The king has promised
Everything we came to ask for. Apollo
The healer, whose priestess gave us good answers
May come himself to cure this sickness
Of man and beast. Let us pray for that.
Exit CREON.
The people disperse and leave the stage.
Enter the CHORUS *of Counsellors of Thebes.*
CHORUS. With a voice sweet as music from the house of gold
The priestess speaks to sunlit Thebes,
And the god speaks through her. But his meaning's obscure.
My hands are shaking, my heart is cold,

On the rack with fear.
From your island of Delos, supreme physician,
Send us your antidote to ease these plagues.
Is this torture unique, or the old condition
Of suffering man through the centuries?
The golden child of hope never dies
And we live by her prophecies.

Ever-living Athene, wise daughter of Zeus,
We sing first to you, and your chaste sister
Artemis, the deer-slayer queen,
Whose stony eyes watch in the market place
From her marble throne:
And bowman Apollo, infallible marksman,
Trinity of deities, show us your power,
Purge our diseases, and save our nation,
If ever you saved us in the days of disaster,
When the plague enforced its reign of terror
And a fire consumed us that no man could master.

Our agonies are beyond telling,
A whole city slowly dying
From an enemy no man can fight.
Slime and fungus on orchard and meadow,
Death in the womb, and birth in the shadow
Of death, and in the mother's sight.
Men die without number, like birds flying,
Like fire consuming, despairing, crying,
As they pass to the shadows of night.

The smell of the dead, the street stinking,
Breeds death and more death, beyond all counting.
No tears as her children die
From the girl wife and the grey-haired mother,
Tearing their nails at the crowded altar,
Accusing the implacable sky.
Healer Apollo, Athene all-knowing,
Can you not hear a whole city screaming,
Will you not answer our cry?

Now let the bloodstained god of war

Whose savage music I hear
Though no swords clash or shields ring,
Be driven from our city, where the only song
Is the groan of the dying, the whimper of fear.
Rout him, the man-slayer, let him fly
In disorder, let him hide his head
In some bleak Thracian bay,
Or ease himself in Amphitrite's bed.
Now, whoever survives the night
Dies at first light.
Great Father Zeus, you who punish with fire,
Incinerate the god of war
Before we all lie dead.

Stand by us now, wolfish god-king,
Pull taut your golden bowstring
And let fly your shaft that never misses:
And hard-riding Artemis, whose torches
Flare on the Lycian slopes, trailing
Sparks as you pass – and god of ecstasy,
Bacchus above all, whose drowsy peace
Inspires and protects our city,
God of the golden turban and flushed face
By your resinous torchlight we stamp and cry
As your Maenads sweep by
From the frenzied east: fly to us, wielding
Ecstatic fire to burn this killing
God, whom the gods themselves despise!

Enter OEDIPUS, *from the palace.*

OEDIPUS. You have prayed to the gods. Now listen to me.
If you act as I tell you to act,
Follow my instructions in every detail
Those prayers will soon be answered.
I speak as an outsider. I know nothing of this story,
The murder or the murderer. So, without your help
And hardly a clue to go on, alone,
What trail can I follow? When the crime was committed
I wasn't even a citizen of Thebes.
So, first, I'll make a public proclamation.
If any man here knows the killer's name,
He must speak out now, in public, to me!

Silence.
Or perhaps one of you is the guilty man?
If that man is here, and gives himself up,
Now, it will be easier for him.
There will be no capital charge.
The severest sentence I shall pronounce
Will be exile. No greater punishment than that.
Silence.
Or maybe one of you has inside knowledge
That some foreigner was the killer?
If you turn informer, you will be well paid,
I shall see to that. But my gratitude
Will be the truest, most satisfying reward.
Silence.
If, however, that man *is* here,
And refuses to speak, or if anyone,
Out of fear for himself, his friends or his family
Ignores these offers, and then is discovered
To be sheltering someone, or himself,
On that man I pass sentence already.
It doesn't matter who he is, I, Oedipus, forbid
Anyone to speak with, or give shelter to that man
In this city, or in the country under my rule.
No man may pray with him, make sacrifices with him,
Nor even allow him to wash in his house!
Every man will kick him out of doors
As the perpetrator of the horrible crime
That brings this suffering on our city! –
According to the prophetic word of Apollo,
As revealed to me, by the Delphic oracle
I stand here as the champion of the god,
And of the dead king too! For the man himself,
The murderer: with all solemnity, I curse him,
Whether he acted alone, or with others,
To bear the mark of this crime for the rest of his life,
Without friends, homeless and in misery!
I'll go further. I don't even exclude myself.
If, knowingly, I should shelter
This criminal in any house or hearth,
Or any place of mine, let the curse I have uttered
Fall on me too, as fiercely as on anyone!

That is my sentence, and it's up to you
To see it fully carried out,
For the god's sake, for my sake,
And the sake of our plague-ridden god-deserted city.
To be honest with you, I am surprised
That no purification ceremonies or investigations
Were undertaken, when so excellent a king
As Laius was inexplicably murdered.
Even without the gods' command
That should have been looked into, I would have thought.
Now, however, I am king.
I enjoy Laius' title, his bed, and his wife:
She is a kind of common ground
Between us, and his children, indeed
If he had had any, would be another bond,
Sharing a mother with mine.
And he was a sad victim of this tragedy.
These links between us, and my feeling for the man,
Make me determined to fight for him now
As if he were my own father. Nothing
Will be too much trouble to ferret him out,
This destroyer of Laius, heir to Labdacus
And all the ancient kings of Thebes,
Back to Cadmus himself, and Agenor, his father.
And if any man dares to disobey these orders,
May all the god's curses fall on him too,
Barren earth, barren cattle,
A barren wife, and all the horrors
This suffering city daily endures,
Without mercy, till the end of his life.
For the honest people of Thebes, who follow me
In intention and action, justice be ours,
And the god's help, today and every day!

CHORUS. That curse would frighten any man,
Great king of Thebes, and it terrifies me!
I'm not the killer. Let me say that at once,
And I can't point him out or tell you his name.
The god Apollo asked this question.
He, if anyone, should tell us the answer.

OEDIPUS. I don't doubt that. But if you can tell me
How a man persuades a god to speak

When the god doesn't want to, I shall thank you for it!
CHORUS. One other thing might be worth saying,
Second best, admittedly.
OEDIPUS. Second best, third best,
Say what you think. Any man's opinion
Is worth hearing at a time like this.
CHORUS. The prophet and astrologer Teiresias
Has studied the mysteries of men and gods:
He has knowledge and experience and insight.
He, more than anyone, could help us now.
OEDIPUS. Which is why I have sent for him already!
Nothing, my friends, has been overlooked.
Creon suggested it. I've sent for him twice
And expected him here some time ago.
CHORUS. There were rumours, of course. Gossip in the market place.
OEDIPUS. Rumours? What rumours? You must tell me everything.
CHORUS. That travellers killed him, somewhere on the road.
OEDIPUS. I've heard that already. There are no witnesses.
CHORUS. But when your curse has been made public
Someone may come forward. Hearing that,
It would take a brave man to keep silent.
OEDIPUS. No murderer fears words, if he can stomach murder.
CHORUS. Here comes the man to tease out the truth:
The blind man, the shaman Teiresias.
He sees into the heart of things,
And has solved more mysteries than any man living.
Enter TEIRESIAS, *blind, led by a boy.*
OEDIPUS. Teiresias! You have made yourself master
Of all the arts of understanding,
Both mystic symbolism and practical wisdom.
The highest spiritual truths, and the most down-to-earth
Material realities are equally your province.
You see the state of our city. Not with your eyes,
I know, but with your intellect.
We rely on you, as our spiritual champion.
We sent to the oracle: you'll have heard that already,
And the answer we were given: find out the killers
Of the old king: execute them, or banish them
And only then will your city be clean.
So, maestro, we need your talents now.

We know that in the formation of birds
In flight, and many other omens,
You can read the future. For your own sake,
For the sake of the city, and for me,
Help us to end this pestilence.
A dead man walks in our streets,
Blinds us with his shadow. We are in your hands.
A gifted man puts his gifts to best use
In the service of his fellow men.
TEIRESIAS. Mine is a terrifying gift. What use
Is wisdom, if it only leads to suffering?
I knew this before I came: and foolishly
Forgot it. I should have stayed at home.
OEDIPUS. That's a gloomy answer! What is it supposed
To mean?
TEIRESIAS. Please let me go home.
Things will be best that way.
You will bear your burden, I will bear mine.
OEDIPUS. Do you refuse to answer my question?
This is Thebes, your country. You were born here!
TEIRESIAS. I've heard your proclamation. It's misconceived:
So it's best for me to keep silent.
OEDIPUS. Dear gods!
Do you mean that you know, and won't say?
Look, look around at us, the whole city!
We are all imploring you to speak.
TEIRESIAS. That is because you are all blind
To what I can see. I can't tell you.
The truth is painful. My secret. And yours.
OEDIPUS. You do know it, don't you! And you're holding back!
Are you prepared to watch the whole country die?
TEIRESIAS. I'm saving you from agony. And myself.
Don't ask me again, don't waste your time.
I shall tell you nothing.
OEDIPUS. Nothing?
What sort of a monster are you? A stone statue
Would be moved to fury, much less a man!
Do you mean this? Are you determined to say nothing?
TEIRESIAS. You lose your temper, make me your scapegoat,
When it's your own anger you should blame.
OEDIPUS. Can you hear him? What this man is saying?

This is an insult to the state,
Every decent citizen will be outraged!

TEIRESIAS. I can't change the future: only describe it.
What will happen, will happen,
Whatever I say.

OEDIPUS. It's your duty.
To say what you know. If *it* must come,
You must tell me!

TEIRESIAS. Lose your temper, shout, stamp, if that pleases you.
I shall say nothing more.

OEDIPUS. Oh yes, I shall be angry,
And more than angry! I understand this much.
I understand that *you* were implicated,
Maybe planned this murder, did everything
But act it: and would have done that too
In my opinion, if you'd had eyes
To see your victim!

TEIRESIAS. Would I indeed?
You compel me to speak. The curse you proclaimed
Is now upon your head: from today
Never to speak to me, or anyone.
You are the man: the unclean thing:
The dirt that breeds disease.

OEDIPUS. Do you dare
To accuse me? Do you slander me
In public, and think your fortune-telling
Gives you some kind of immunity?

TEIRESIAS. I don't need it. The truth is its own protector.

OEDIPUS. Someone's behind this. Who told you to say that?
There's more to this than fortune-telling.

TEIRESIAS. You did. You made me say it. Against my will.

OEDIPUS. Say it again. So there will be no doubt.

TEIRESIAS. Didn't you hear? Or do you want me to elaborate?

OEDIPUS. I heard. But I didn't believe my ears.
Say it again. Aloud. To everybody.

TEIRESIAS. You are the murderer of the murdered king.

OEDIPUS. Twice! To my face! You will regret this, old man.

TEIRESIAS. Indulge your anger if it pleases you.
I could say more, to make you angrier still.

OEDIPUS. Why not! More lunacy! Let's have it all!

TEIRESIAS. I know, but you do not,

That the woman you love is not the woman you love,
That the relationship is disgusting, taboo,
And, in your ignorance, will destroy you.

OEDIPUS. Do you expect to say such things and not be punished?

TEIRESIAS. The truth protects me, if I tell it honestly.

OEDIPUS. The truth? What's the truth to you?
You're blind all over, ears, mind, as well as eyes.

TEIRESIAS. I pity you. People will scream the same insults
At you, before long. Everyone will despise you.

OEDIPUS. You live in darkness, permanently,
You see nothing of the real world!
My eyes are open. You can't hurt me.

TEIRESIAS. How could I? An old man. It's not my business.
Apollo will do it. It's in his hands.

OEDIPUS. Creon! Of course! *He* went to the oracle!
This plot is his doing, not yours.

TEIRESIAS. Creon isn't your enemy. You are.

OEDIPUS. Political rank, wealth and power,
And men's ambitions clawing at each other,
Till life becomes a battleground,
And envy everyone's motive!
Creon is, and has been my friend.
I've trusted him completely. This crown
Was given to me, freely, by the people,
I didn't ask for it. And this man,
My friend, is secretly plotting to overthrow me
With a spiritual quack, a charlatan,
A paranormal stuntman, whose eyes
Are stone blind when it comes to prophesy,
But where money's concerned, very sharp,
Wide open then! Astrology,
Fortune-telling, forecasting the future,
Where was all that when we needed it?
There was a monster here – do you remember?
I'm sure you do – with the face of a woman
And the body of a dog, who terrorised this city.
Where were you then? What was your advice
To save this country? She set a riddle
Which no ordinary man could answer. Someone special
Was required. What else are prophets for?
But you hadn't a clue, had you!

Not a word, not the slightest suggestion!
And then I came along, a young man,
Quite ignorant, knowing nothing, with only the wit
My mother gave me. But I stopped her mouth.
I did it, Oedipus! I guessed her riddle,
Without any gobbledygook about birds!
And I, Oedipus, I am the man
You hope to depose, you and Creon,
So that he will be king, and you his guru.
Well. You will regret it. You will both regret
This attempt to turn me into a scapegoat.
If you weren't an old man, punishment would teach you
The difference between prophecy and sedition.

CHORUS. Great king,
To speak in anger, as both of you have done,
Helps none of us, as far as I can judge,
When our city is dying. We must consider
The god's command, and how to obey it.

TEIRESIAS. You may be king, but I am a free man,
And I have the right to answer. I serve
Apollo, the god, not you, nor Creon.
You sneer at my blindness. You have eyes,
But cannot see your own corruption.
Nor who she is you love the most,
Not even whose son you are. In your ignorance
You have committed terrible crimes
Against those closest to you, the living,
And the dead. A double curse,
Like a two-edged sword, father and mother,
Will drive you from this city, into exile,
For ever, and what a cripple you'll be then.
Those bright eyes, that perfect vision
You are so proud of, will become dark,
Like mine. There will be no place on earth
That hasn't heard the sound of your pain.
The wildest heathland of Cithaeron,
Even its cliffs and ravines, will echo
To your bellowing, when you understand
How those melodious marriage songs
Deceived you, when they led you
To that safe harbour you imagined here.

Then unimaginable sufferings, miseries
You cannot guess at, will become familiar
Both to you, and to your children
As you pile your agonies upon their heads.
Accuse Creon of every crime.
Slander him, despise what I say.
Every man in the world will despise you,
And no man has committed crimes like yours.

OEDIPUS. I don't have to listen to you! Why should I?
Get him out of my sight, now, at once,
Take him back where he came from.

TEIRESIAS. Yes.
I shall go now. You brought me here,
Remember that. I didn't want to come.

OEDIPUS. If I'd known what I'd have to listen to,
The ravings of a lunatic,
Believe me, I'd have left you in peace.

TEIRESIAS. You think I was born a fool. Your parents
Wouldn't think so.

OEDIPUS. Why this continual harping
Upon my parents? Who . . . fathered me?

TEIRESIAS. Today you will father your own destruction
And conceive the truth of your birth and death.

OEDIPUS. Speak plainly, don't talk in riddles.

TEIRESIAS. Why not! You have a genius for solving them.

OEDIPUS. Yes, I'm famous for it. And your sneers and insults
Won't make me any the less incisive.

TEIRESIAS. That fame is your misfortune.

OEDIPUS. I saved the state.
With my genius. What does it matter to me
What you choose to call it?

TEIRESIAS. Now I shall go.
Give me your hand, boy. Take me home.

OEDIPUS. Yes, take him and good riddance. We can do without you.
Rave in your own house and spare mine.

TEIRESIAS. I'll go. I've said what I came to say,
And I've said it to your face. Why should I be frightened?
You no longer have the power to hurt me.
But I will say one thing more. The man
You're looking for, the man you cursed
And threatened, the murderer of Laius,

Is here. He passes for a foreigner,
Who lives in Thebes. But he was born here,
And will learn that, to his cost.
He could see when he came here. He'll leave blind.
He's a rich man now. He will go as a beggar.
Groping, with a stick in his hand,
Tapping his way, he will leave this city,
Into endless exile. To his children,
Whom he loves, he is brother and father:
To the woman who bore him, lover and son.
To his father, a killer and the man who supplants him.
Go in. Set your genius to solve those riddles.
Call me a blind man, when you've proved them untrue.

TEIRESIAS *signs to the boy, who leads him away.* OEDIPUS *watches him, then turns and moves, angrily, back into the palace.*

CHORUS. Who is this man whose terrible crime
The unearthly voice of Apollo's vessel
Intones from the rock of Delphi?
Far let that man fly,
For his hands trail blood, from a sin the oracle
Blushes to whisper. Faster than the storm
His horse must run, outstrip the wind;
Thundering Zeus' son gallops behind,
Grasped in his fist the lethal lightning,
And the hounds of the gods,
The unsleeping Fates,
Close in, like a circle tightening.

From the snowbound crest of Parnassus the word
Was transmitted to Thebes: you must find this killer
Lurking like a thief in the night;
Drag him into the light!
Like a mountain bull where the forests are thicker,
The caves bleaker, he creeps, barred
From the company of men, hopelessly flies
The voice of those bleak prophecies
That buzz and sting at his face. No distance
From earth's centrepoint,
Delphi's sacred summit,
Is too far for Apollo's vengeance.

Teiresias has spread fear and confusion.
Should we believe him or not? For us,
Best to keep quiet. I'm like jelly, uncertain
What's happening, or will happen. Was there ever a row
In the past, or is there now,
Between Polybus' son and the ruling line
Of Thebes, the house of Labdacus?
Not that I ever heard.
What could be more absurd
Than to blacken – with no proof – Oedipus' name
By pinning this unsolved murder on him?

The secrets of man, all the mysteries of his nature,
Are known to Zeus and Apollo. No one
Can claim a monopoly of wisdom. One teacher
Is as good as another, and perhaps no better
Than any of us. Some may see deeper,
And some may not, because wisdom is a jointure
Unequally shared among men. But what was done
Must be known, beyond doubt.
Oedipus saved our state;
He publicly outwitted the Sphinx. Like gold,
He was tested and found true. We must see his guilt proved!
Enter CREON, *from the direction of the city.*
CREON. Citizens! Members of the council. They tell me
That the king has charged me with subversion!
I am innocent of any such charge. The city
Is on its knees. Does he imagine
At a time like this I would injure him
By any word or action? I'd rather die
Than be smeared like that! It is a smear,
To be accused of treason, before you
And my friends and my countrymen.
CHORUS. He lost his temper and made wild accusations.
I think he spoke without thought.
CREON. Did he say
That the old prophet lied, under my instructions?
Who gave him that idea?
CHORUS. He did say it:
But why he said it, or whether he meant it
Is a matter of opinion.

CREON. Is he right in the head?
Did he speak rationally and look you in the eye,
Or has he gone mad?
CHORUS. I've got more common sense
Than to make judgements like that on a king's actions.
Here he comes from the palace, he'll speak for himself.
Enter OEDIPUS, *from the palace.*
OEDIPUS. So you're here, Creon! What have you come for?
I hardly thought you would be thick-skinned enough
To come knocking at my doors again,
While you're planning to murder me and steal my power.
Do you imagine I'm afraid of you? Or stupid?
Or am I just too blind to notice
A conspiracy to overthrow me? Or not bright enough
To do anything about it? And what a conspiracy!
You need plenty of friends and financial backing
To capture a throne. Revolutions are made
With men, and the money to pay them, or buy them.
CREON. Can I speak in my own defence? Judge me
After you've heard my answer, not before!
OEDIPUS. Creon, you've always been a brilliant talker.
But talk cuts no ice with me. I've seen
The evidence of your actions, betrayal,
Sedition . . .
CREON. Will you let me speak?
OEDIPUS. Say what you like. But don't protest
Your innocence, that would be too much!
CREON. Do you really believe that closing your mind –
A boneheaded refusal to listen –
Is a sensible way of proceeding?
OEDIPUS. Do you really believe that I can allow you
To plot a palace revolution, and do nothing about it,
Because you are my brother-in-law?
CREON. Only a fool would allow that, I agree,
If it were happening! There is no revolution,
In the palace, or anywhere. No conspiracy!
What am I supposed to have done?
OEDIPUS. It was you
Advised me to send for that canting prophet.
CREON. Yes it was. Good advice. I'd give it again.
OEDIPUS. Tell me. How long ago did Laius . . . ?

CREON. Did Laius what? I don't follow you.
OEDIPUS. He died mysteriously. How long ago was that?
CREON. Years and years. I can hardly remember.
OEDIPUS. And this fortune-teller. He was here then,
Already in the prophecy business?
CREON. Respected then as now, for his skill and integrity.
OEDIPUS. And did he mention me when the murder happened?
CREON. Not in my hearing.
OEDIPUS. And there was no inquest,
Nor any kind of investigation?
CREON. There was an inquiry. But it revealed nothing
OEDIPUS. This respected prophet. Why did he say nothing
Then, of what he has said today?
CREON. I've no idea. I never say anything
Unless I'm in full possession of the facts.
OEDIPUS. But one thing you do know and you'd be wise to tell me.
CREON. What can I say? Everything I know
I will tell you. I'll keep nothing back.
OEDIPUS. You know this much. Without your prompting
The fortune-teller would never have dared
To accuse *me* of the murder of Laius!
CREON. Did he say that? . . . Then you must know
If he's lying or telling the truth; not I.
Am I permitted to interrogate you?
OEDIPUS. Why not? I've got nothing to hide.
You will never pin this murder on me.
CREON. Are you married to my sister?
OEDIPUS. What sort
Of question's that? I can hardly
Deny it, can I. I do have that honour.
CREON. She shares the throne, both title and revenue?
OEDIPUS. Of course she does. What's mine is hers.
CREON. And I'm the third partner? I have my share
Of power and responsibility?
OEDIPUS. You've always had it. All the more disgusting
To conspire against me behind your back!
CREON. But I haven't conspired against you! Ask yourself,
As I ask myself, whether any sane man
Would willingly exchange a quiet life
Within the ruling family, for the wear and tear,
The gruelling responsibility of government?

It has never crossed my mind. I have no ambition
To be king in name, or in fact.
I live like a king. Sometimes, I hope,
I act like one. And that's enough.
No sensible man would want more than that.
If I had your job, there'd be too many things
I wouldn't like doing: and no more satisfaction
From the kingship itself, than I get now
From royal rank, without royal obligation.
I'm not so drunk with the prospect of power
As to envy a position that yields no profit.
Look at me now. Everyone knows me,
Everyone loves me, I think. Anyone who hopes
To get your attention, first tries for mine,
Because my influence guarantees success.
Why should I change such a favourable situation?
Is it likely that I'd be such a fool
As to break with you in such conditions,
As far as to commit treason? As a political policy
It has nothing to recommend it. It's not mine,
Nor the policy of any of my friends,
Not if I know them. If you want proof,
Send to the priestess at the oracle;
Check the message I brought, if it was true!
Produce some evidence of conspiracy
Between the blind man and me. Prove that,
And condemn me to death, out of hand.
My verdict, in those conditions,
Will be as merciless as any man's.
But to condemn me like this, on mere suspicion,
Without any evidence! I can't endure that!
It is unjust to condemn people with no good reason.
If mere supposition, unsupported,
Is all your evidence, you can call bad men honest
And decent citizens crooks and villains,
And justice will be done to none of them!
A reliable friend is a precious possession,
Worth a man's life. Throw friendship away,
You destroy something living and irreplaceable.
The truth of this will emerge in time.
Time is the one incorruptible judge.

One minute is long enough to accuse a man.
To prove his innocence takes longer.

CHORUS. If you weigh his words, they make good sense,
Well worth a prudent man's consideration.
Quick judgements are not always the wisest.

OEDIPUS. Conspiracies don't take their time,
They keep on the move! And counter-intelligence
Must move fast too, or be caught napping!
Shall I sit and do nothing while he takes power
And my own sluggishness destroys me?

CREON. What do you want then? To have me banished?

OEDIPUS. Banished? Oh no, I want you dead.

CREON. What have I done to provoke such jealousy?

OEDIPUS. Are you still so obstinate, still pretending?

CREON. Yes I am. Because you're not thinking straight.

OEDIPUS. I know where my best interests lie.

CREON. But what about mine?

OEDIPUS. You are a traitor.

CREON. And you are mistaken.

OEDIPUS. Kings must take decisions.

CREON. Not wrong decisions.

OEDIPUS. O Thebes, my city –

CREON. Thebes is my city as well as yours!

CHORUS. Princes, stop this brawling. The queen, Jocasta,
Is coming from the palace, not a moment too soon.
She will help us to put an end to this quarrel.

Enter JOCASTA, *from the palace.*

JOCASTA. What is all this shouting? From inside the palace
I heard angry voices, like a quarrel.
Aren't you ashamed, indulging yourselves
In private arguments, squabbling like boys
While the city dies all around you? Go inside,
My husband – and you too, Creon, go back
To your own house, before you make
A private row into a public spectacle.

CREON. Sister, we are blood relations! But your husband
Has condemned me, unheard, to the choice
Of death or exile!

OEDIPUS. Certainly I have,
And that, dear wife, is the least I can do!

CREON. May all the gods curse me for ever

If I was even remotely guilty!
JOCASTA. Oedipus, you must believe him. An oath
Like that can't be taken lightly.
Believe him, for my sake, and for the sake
Of these reliable counsellors. They heard it all.
CHORUS. Great king, be prepared to change your mind.
OEDIPUS. Are you asking me to break my word?
CHORUS. No man ever questioned his integrity.
He confirms it by oath. Show some leniency.
OEDIPUS. Do you know what you're asking?
CHORUS. Certainly we do.
OEDIPUS. Say it openly then. Let everyone know.
CHORUS. He's your long-trusted friend, above suspicion.
Don't condemn him by hearsay, and in spite of his oath.
OEDIPUS. Don't you understand my own implication?
Spare *him*, and you demand *my* banishment or death!
CHORUS. By the life-giving sun, that necessary power
By whose warmth we live, such a terrible thought
Never crossed my mind! I had far rather
Be an outcast, godless, friendless, distraught
And despised, than embrace that destiny.
Our city is in anguish. What greater blow
Could fall on us in our misery
Than anger and hatred between you two?
OEDIPUS. Then let him go.
Even if my death, exile and disgrace
Is the price of your mercy. Your voice buys his pardon,
Not his. Wherever he hides his face
Let my backbreaking hatred be his burden.
CREON. Your apology's as graceless as your anger's insane.
An unforgiving nature breeds misery
In its own heart, not that of its enemy.
OEDIPUS. Leave me in peace! I want you gone!
CREON. Yes, I'll go. They respect my integrity.
I am misjudged by you alone.
Exit CREON.
CHORUS. Take the king inside, madam. Speak to him in private.
JOCASTA. What caused this quarrel? Who began it?
CHORUS. Rumours were mentioned, unfounded suspicions:
Then the anger that follows unjust accusations.
JOCASTA. Both men were at fault then?

CHORUS. Yes, madam, they were.
JOCASTA. Tell me all the details. You can speak without fear.
CHORUS. We have troubles enough, best to keep silent.
In all our interests, let sleeping dogs lie.
OEDIPUS. Your intentions are honourable, but your advice is pregnant
With disaster. All the guilt falls on me!
CHORUS. Great king, believe me when I say again
What I've said before: we would be stark-mad
To counsel an action so insane
As to cast you out without proof. We need
Your help and guidance. We all remember
How like a pilot in that desperate storm,
Half-wrecked, you navigated us to harbour.
You are our captain, in rough weather or calm.
JOCASTA. Please tell me. What harm
Can Creon have done to provoke such fury
So suddenly? I am worthy of your trust.
OEDIPUS. These old men mean well. But you matter to me
Far more. It's Creon. I'm sickened with disgust
At the scope of his conspiracy.
JOCASTA. What conspiracy? And why do you accuse my brother?
OEDIPUS. He says I'm responsible for Laius' murder.
JOCASTA. Has he any evidence? Or is it hearsay?
OEDIPUS. He says nothing himself. That corrupt fortune-teller
Speaks for him, with his bird-talk and prophecy!

JOCASTA. And is that all? Set your mind at rest.
No one can forecast the future. I know
What I'm talking about, from personal experience.
I have proof! When Laius was alive
An oracle told him – I won't say the god spoke,
But his mouthpiece did – that he would be killed
By his own son – our own child.
But it didn't happen. Laius was killed
By persons unknown, foreign robbers –
According to the story – at a place
Where three roads meet. As for the child,
It was abandoned on a deserted mountain
Before it was three days old, by a servant.
To make doubly sure, its ankles were pierced

And strapped together with leather thongs.
So *that* prediction didn't come true,
In spite of Apollo. That prophecy of parricide
Wasn't fulfilled. Laius was murdered,
But not, as he feared, by his own son.
The oracle had been unambiguous,
Its meaning quite plain. So why take notice
Of these fortune-tellers and astrologers?
The gods always get their own way,
Without anyone's help, when they are ready.

OEDIPUS. Something you said Jocasta . . . I remember . . .
My brain's a turmoil . . . feelings, memories . . .

JOCASTA. Why do you look at me so strangely? What's the matter?

OEDIPUS. You said, didn't you, that Laius was butchered
At a place where three roads meet?

JOCASTA. Yes,
That was said at the time. It's still
The common story.

OEDIPUS. Where? What country?

JOCASTA. A place in Phocis, at the junction
Where the road from Thebes forks to Daulia and Delphi.

OEDIPUS. And how long ago did all this happen?

JOCASTA. You hadn't arrived. The news became public
A short while before you became king.

OEDIPUS. Oh Zeus . . . What will you do to me?

JOCASTA. Oedipus . . . you look terrified. What have I said?

OEDIPUS. Not yet. Don't ask me yet. How old
Was Laius? What kind of man was he?

JOCASTA. A big man.
Hair greying. About your build.

OEDIPUS. Dear God. Without knowing it
I may have damned myself. Just a moment ago.

JOCASTA. Don't look at me like that! What do you mean?

OEDIPUS. Maybe Teiresias could see after all:
Terrifying, but possible. Tell me one more thing.

JOCASTA. Why are you frightening me? I'll tell you everything.

OEDIPUS. Who was with the king? A few attendants,
Or was he travelling in state, with servants and armed men?

JOCASTA. Five men, all told. One of them a herald.
Laius himself rode in a carriage.

OEDIPUS. Ahh . . .

Nothing could be clearer than that. Every detail.
Where did you get this information?

JOCASTA. There was one survivor, a servant. Eventually
He got back to Thebes.

OEDIPUS. Is he still here now?

JOCASTA. No he isn't. By the time he got back
Everything had changed in the city,
And you were king in Laius' place.
When he saw how things were, he came to me
And begged me on his knees to let him go
Away to the country, to be a shepherd.
He said he wanted to be done with Thebes,
Out of sight, out of mind. So I let him go.
He was a good servant and deserved better than that.

OEDIPUS. I want him here at once, today.
Can we find him?

JOCASTA. Of course we can.
Why are you so anxious?

OEDIPUS. My dear wife, I'm frightened,
Of what I've done – what I'm doing.
I've already said far too much.
I must see this shepherd. Ask him some questions.

JOCASTA. You will see him. We'll send for him.
But why are you so worried? You must tell me.
I do have a right to know.

OEDIPUS. Yes, yes.
You have a right to know. If the truth
Of this is what I think it is,
No one has a better right to know
Than you. I'll tell you the whole story.
My father, Polybus, was Corinth-born,
And Merope, my mother, came from Doris.
I was an up-and-coming fellow,
Very much the man to watch, until one day
An odd thing happened: an astonishing thing
Which caused more trouble perhaps than it merited,
But which I took seriously. At a banquet one day,
A man who had drunk too much jeered at me,
And said I was not my father's son.
I was very hurt, angry and insulted,
But I kept it to myself for the rest of that day.

The next morning I went to my parents,
Father and mother together, and asked them
Question after question, almost compelling them
To tell me the truth. They were very angry
That anyone should dare say such a thing,
And put my mind at rest as best they could.
But a thing like that gets under your skin.
I couldn't forget it. And the story
Got around a good deal as these things do.
So, without telling my parents, I went
To the oracle at Delphi. I got no answer
To the question I asked: a catalogue
Of horrors and miseries instead – that I
Would marry my own mother, and father
Children on her, conceived incestuously,
And become a public outcast for it, notorious
Throughout the world. As if this weren't enough,
I would kill my own father. What could I do?
I ran, as fast and as far from Corinth
As any man could, always checking
My distance from that forbidden city
By the positions of the stars: so that those dreadful prophecies
Could not possibly come true. The route
I took brought me into that part of the country
Where, according to you, Laius was murdered.
Now listen Jocasta, this is the truth
In every detail. I reached a place
Where three roads meet. At the junction,
I was confronted by a herald, ahead of a carriage
Drawn by horses and carrying a passenger,
Just as you described, grey-haired, my build.
The man in front shouted at me
To clear the road, and the old man too
Rudely ordered me to get out of his way.
The driver barged into me, so I hit him
Hard. I was furious by now, uncontrollable.
The old man in the carriage was watching for his chance.
He waited till I passed him. And then, he struck me
Full on the head with his two-pronged stick –
The kind you use for goading the horses
To make them gallop. I paid him back

With interest, and double quick.
I whacked him, savagely, with my staff,
And knocked him out of the carriage. He fell
Flat in the road. The others attacked me,
Of course. And I killed them. Every one.
Now if that old man was remotely connected
With Laius – if the king's blood
Ran in his veins – is there any man
On earth more miserable than I am?
Every god will hate me, and all men.
No one will speak to me, friend or stranger,
No one will take me into his house.
I cursed the murderer. And the weight of that curse
Now falls on me. These same hands
That killed him have fondled his wife!
Was I cursed from the beginning then, a filthy
Corrupted thing infecting the city,
Deserving exile if anyone deserves it?
Now I am cast out from Thebes, denied
The sight of my wife and children, forbidden
Ever to return to my home in Corinth.
No. Never again can I go back there,
For fear that the oracle might be fulfilled,
And that I should somehow marry my mother
And kill my father Polybus, who nurtured me,
And gave me life. The immortals, I suppose,
Have devised this inhuman scenario
To amuse themselves. But listen, gods,
As you revel in the purity of your power
Over human affairs, I shall do my best
To deprive you of that pleasure. Never,
Never will that day come, if I can prevent it.
I'd rather die, with every memory
Of my existence blotted out
From the face of the earth, than live to see
Such dreadful things come true, and be shamed,
Branded and notorious before humanity.

CHORUS. Your story is terrifying, great king.
But don't give up hope. There was an eye-witness.
Until you've questioned him, say nothing.

OEDIPUS. The shepherd is my last chance.

I'll cling to that.

JOCASTA. Even when he gets here,
What possible help can he be?

OEDIPUS. One detail,
And it's crucial. If his story
Corroborates yours, I am proved innocent.

JOCASTA. What detail? Does it matter? What did I say?

OEDIPUS. In your version of the shepherd's evidence
The king was killed by robbers. Robbers,
Plural. If he says the same,
Still calls them robbers, I'm in the clear.
One man is not a group of men.
Plural is plural, not singular.
But if he describes a single traveller,
Walking alone, then quite obviously
All the evidence will point to me.

JOCASTA. Oh, but he did say that, I'm certain.
He can't change his story now, he spoke
In public, the whole city heard him!
And even if his evidence varies in detail,
By no stretch of the imagination can he pretend
That Laius died as predicted. A child
Of mine would kill him, the oracle said.
And it didn't happen. My poor little boy
Killed no one. He was the one who died
Years before any of this happened.
That's how much oracles are worth. In future
Whatever they say one way or the other
I won't waste my time with any of them!

OEDIPUS. That's the truth of the matter. But we'll speak to the shepherd.
Send someone to fetch him. Now, this minute.

JOCASTA. At once, we'll get him at once! Come inside.
I'll do nothing without your approval. Nothing.

Exeunt OEDIPUS *and* JOCASTA, *into the palace.*

CHORUS. I only ask for an honest life,
And justice, and belief in the moral law,
As the gods decree it
From the ancient summit
Of Olympus, the sacred mountain.
No man made those precepts, they never sleep

Nor decay with age, as men decay.
They run their courses
From immortal sources
Like a pure and eternal fountain.

Arrogant self-love breeds absolute rule,
The tyrant, who eats up money and men.
He seeks absolute power
And in one foolish hour
Overreaches himself, and ends in the gutter.
An ambitious man most honours the gods
When his demon drives him to serve the state.
He sets his store
By the moral law.
The gods love him, and his people prosper.

But what if a man should laugh at justice,
Grab what he wants and disregard,
By his words and actions, honesty and truth,
And plunder holy shrines?
Can he hope to escape
The consequences of his rape?
When the criminal makes off with his loot
And the murderer becomes king,
Why should I still cling
To the old wisdom and morality,
Or honour in song the sacred harmony?

And why should I make pilgrimages
To Delphi and Olympia,
Or any holy place, if these manifest truths
Are not made absolute for every man,
And the gods' warnings provoke laughter
With no thought of what comes after?
Oh Zeus universal, if you hear our song,
Show us again your immortal power
In this darkest hour,
When Laius' fate and Apollo's word
Are both forgotten, and your warnings unheard.

Enter JOCASTA *from the palace, attended by women, who carry incense and garlands of flowers.*

JOCASTA *is disturbed, and moves towards a small stone altar.*

JOCASTA. I have decided, senators of Thebes,
To visit the holiest temples of the city
To make sacrifices there, with incense and flowers,
To the all-powerful gods. The king is confused
At the moment, by his own nightmares and fantasies.
He can't make balanced judgements, or estimate
From past experience what is likely to happen.
Each new sensational revelation
He takes as truth, and is terrified the more.
I've tried to comfort him. But I failed.
So it seemed sensible to offer prayers,
And first to Apollo, whose altar stands nearest.

As she invokes the god, the women lay the offerings on the altar.

Brilliant god of sunlight and healing,
We live in the shadow of a curse. Shine
On our darkest corners, where there is sickness
And dirt, make us whole and clean.
Like desperate sailors, we lose our last hope
When we see our captain in despair.

Enter a Messenger from Corinth.

CORINTHIAN. Gentlemen! Can anyone show me the way
To the palace of King Oedipus? Or better still,
To the man himself, if you know where he is?

CHORUS. This is the palace, and the king is inside it.
This lady is his wife, and mother of his children.

CORINTHIAN. God bless her then, and all her family,
Bearing children to such a great man!

JOCASTA. God bless you too, sir, and thank you
For such a courteous greeting. Have you travelled here
For your own purposes, or to bring us news?

CORINTHIAN. News, dear lady, good news too
For your husband, and for his whole family.

JOCASTA. What news is it? Who sent you?

CORINTHIAN. I come from Corinth, and my message
Is bound to please you: though it's painful too,
And will make you sad to begin with.

JOCASTA. One message
Causing two such opposite reactions? Tell me.

CORINTHIAN. The Corinthians will make Oedipus king
Of the whole isthmus. Everybody says so!

JOCASTA. But Polybus rules in Corinth, and has done
For years. Isn't he still king?
CORINTHIAN. Polybus is dead, my lady, and buried.
JOCASTA. Polybus is dead? The father of Oedipus
Dead?
CORINTHIAN. Unless I'm a liar. In which case
Strike me dead on the spot!
JOCASTA. You girl, quickly,
Go to the king, tell him the news!
Oh, oracles, dreamers of dreams,
Fortune-tellers, where are your predictions now?
The one man Oedipus has kept clear of
For all these years, for fear he should murder him!
And that man's dead, at long last,
Dead! And Oedipus had nothing to do with it!
Enter OEDIPUS *from the palace.*
OEDIPUS. Jocasta? My dearest. You called me out
From the palace again? What's going on?
JOCASTA. This man has news for you. Listen,
And then tell me what you think of oracles
With their mystification and mumbo-jumbo!
OEDIPUS. Who is he? What does he have to say?
JOCASTA. He comes from Corinth. Your father. He's dead.
Polybus. Do you understand? He's dead!
OEDIPUS. What! Tell me yourself! Get it quite clear.
CORINTHIAN. I can't put it any plainer. He's dead all right.
He's gone the way we all go.
OEDIPUS. How did he die? Was it murder, or sickness?
CORINTHIAN. Sleep comes easily to an old man's eyes.
OEDIPUS. He was ill, then, and gradually declined? Poor old man.
CORINTHIAN. He was old, and tired. He'd lived long enough.
OEDIPUS. Well then! Ha! What now, Jocasta?
That priestess at Delphi, and her oracle,
A whole skyful of screaming birds
Prophesying ruin! I was the man
Who would kill my father! And my sword
Has never left its scabbard! Maybe
He died of a broken heart, because I
Was in exile? Maybe I killed him that way!
But I don't think so. Polybus is dead.
And so is the oracle and its prophecies,

Dead and rotten!
JOCASTA. And that was my prophecy.
Didn't I say so, right from the beginning!
OEDIPUS. You said it, but I was confused and frightened.
JOCASTA. Forget it now. It's over
OEDIPUS. My mother.
While she's still alive, I can't be safe.
There's still that to fear.
JOCASTA. Fear? Why fear?
We live our lives at the mercy of chance,
The purest coincidence. No one can predict
The future, so what is the point of fearing it?
Live! Enjoy life! Take each day as it comes!
As for marrying your mother, you're not the first
To have dreamed that dream; every son
Is his mother's lover in imagination
Or in day-dreams. It's commonplace.
If a man broods on his most private fantasies
His life won't be worth living, believe me!
OEDIPUS. All very well, your celebrations,
If the woman who brought me into the world
Happened to be dead too. But she isn't,
Not yet. She's alive. And while she lives
Somewhere inside me I'm still afraid.
JOCASTA. But much less afraid. Your father's dead.
OEDIPUS. Less afraid maybe. Still afraid of her.
CORINTHIAN. Don't mind me asking, sir. Who is this lady
Who scares you so much?
OEDIPUS. The queen, Merope,
The dead king's wife.
CORINTHIAN. What's she done? There's nothing
To scare you about her, surely.
OEDIPUS. My friend, there was an oracle once, from Delphi,
A dreadful prophecy.
CORINTHIAN. Too dreadful
To tell a stranger? Or can anyone hear it?
OEDIPUS. It's no secret. Apollo's mouthpiece,
The Pythia herself, told me I was doomed
To marry my own mother, and kill
My father, bloodily, with my own hands.
It was for that reason I left Corinth,

And have stayed away so long. I've prospered,
As you see, abroad. But nothing can compensate
For the loss of my parents' love, the pleasure,
Denied me, of seeing them face to face.

CORINTHIAN. And that's the fear that's kept you in exile,
No other reason?

OEDIPUS. It was enough.
I was determined not to kill my father.

CORINTHIAN. Well, I came to do you one good turn,
And now I can do you another.

OEDIPUS. What other?
If you know more, you'll earn my gratitude.

CORINTHIAN. That was, partly, my motive in coming,
I will admit. And to do myself
A good turn later, when you come back home.

OEDIPUS. Home? You mean Corinth? I shall never go back.
I shall never see either of my parents again.

CORINTHIAN. My dear young fellow. You've got it all wrong.

OEDIPUS. What do you mean, old man, for god's sake tell me!
Tell me everything you know!

CORINTHIAN. This fear
Of yours, that stops you coming home . . .

OEDIPUS. The fear that the god's prediction should come true . . .

CORINTHIAN. Is it all about your parents
And the crime you're doomed to commit . . . ?

OEDIPUS. Of course it is. And from the very first moment
That fear has never left me.

CORINTHIAN. Pointless
Sir, quite without basis. Nothing to be scared of
At all.

OEDIPUS. Why? I don't understand you.
If I'm their son . . . ?

CORINTHIAN. Who says you're their son?
Polybus wasn't your father. No relation
At all.

OEDIPUS. What are you saying? Polybus
Was not my father?

CORINTHIAN. No more your father
Than I am. Just the same relationship in fact.

OEDIPUS. The same relationship, my father and you?
How is that possible?

CORINTHIAN. It's possible because
That man was not your father and neither
Am I.
OEDIPUS. Then why did he call me his son?
CORINTHIAN. I gave you to him. As a present.
OEDIPUS. Gave me to him? But he loved me
Like a son, no father could have done more!
CORINTHIAN. He had no children: and wanted a child.
OEDIPUS. What was I then? A foundling? Or a slave-child,
Bought somewhere?
CORINTHIAN. Not a bit of it!
You were found, on the mountain, in a hollow
Under some trees. Up there, on Cithaeron!
OEDIPUS. And what were *you* doing up there?
CORINTHIAN. Looking after the sheep. That was my job.
OEDIPUS. What were you, a journeyman shepherd
Taking whatever work came?
CORINTHIAN. That's right.
And a good job for you that I was, eh? Son?
Because I saved your life. No question about that!
OEDIPUS. Was I in danger then? Or in pain?
CORINTHIAN. In pain! Look at your ankles! They're still
Swollen up, more than normal.
OEDIPUS. What's that
To do with it? An old weakness
I've had since a child.
CORINTHIAN. I know you have!
Your ankles were drilled through and tied together!
I cut you free!
OEDIPUS. That must be true.
You can still see the scars. I had them as a boy.
CORINTHIAN. How else did you get your name? 'Oedipus.'
'Swollen Foot'! That's what it means, doesn't it?
OEDIPUS. Dear gods, who would do such a thing to a child?
My father, or my mother?
CORINTHIAN. Don't ask me that!
Ask the other chap, the one who gave you to me.
OEDIPUS. Gave me? You didn't find me yourself?
CORINTHIAN. I did not. There was another shepherd.
He asked me to look after you.
OEDIPUS. And who was he? Could you identify him?

CORINTHIAN. He was always thought of as one of Laïus' men.
OEDIPUS. Laius? The Laius who was king here before?
CORINTHIAN. King Laius, that's the one. This chap worked for him.
OEDIPUS. Is he still alive? Where can I see him?
CORINTHIAN. Ask your own people. They should know.
OEDIPUS. This shepherd . . . Good people, do any of you know him,
Has anyone seen him, here, or in the country?
If you know this man, for god's sake, say!
Speak out, now! The time has come
To solve this mystery, once and for all!
CHORUS. I think this shepherd, and the other shepherd
You've already sent for, must be identical.
But ask the queen. She's sure to know.
OEDIPUS. Jocasta, you know this shepherd, the one
We've sent for. Is it the same man?

JOCASTA *is white with fear, hardly able to reply.*

JOCASTA. What man . . . ? What does it matter . . . One shepherd or another . . .
What difference does it make? None of it matters.
Forget it. The whole thing. Don't pursue it.
OEDIPUS. Forget it! Of course I can't forget it!
What nonsense! My birth's a mystery,
But with all these clues, I intend to solve it!
JOCASTA. Listen to me in heaven's name,
Listen. If you want to stay alive
This search must end. It's making me ill
I'm sick with it already, isn't that enough?
OEDIPUS. There's no need for such gloom! Suppose it proved
I was born a slave, from generations of slaves,
Would that sicken you? Or affect your standing?
JOCASTA. Listen, I'm begging you! Don't go on!
OEDIPUS. I must go on! I must know the truth!
JOCASTA. I know! I know what I'm talking about.
I'm telling you this for your own good.
OEDIPUS. And when did I ever put my own good,
As you call it, before the service of the state?
JOCASTA. My god, you're doomed, you can't escape!
I have one wish, and one wish only:
That you never discover who you really are.
OEDIPUS. Hurry, one of you! Get that shepherd here!

My wife is too proud of her blue blood.
She's scared she may have married a slave!
JOCASTA. It's finished. No chance now. You're doomed.
I've said all there is to say:
And my last word to you. For ever.

JOCASTA *goes into the palace.*

CHORUS. Why has the queen left us so suddenly?
Why did she become so emotional?
I don't like it, this refusal to speak.
It's like the silence that hangs over a city
When a storm is about to break.
OEDIPUS. Storms, hurricanes, let them all come!
I've travelled this far, and now I'm determined
To discover my identity. If my birthplace
Was the gutter, I shall hunt it out!
My wife, like all women, is snobbish
About rank and upbringing. If I was the child
Of chance, with good luck for my godparents,
I wouldn't be ashamed. My true mother
Is fortunate coincidence, my brothers and sisters
The changing seasons, and I change with them
As naturally as the trees. If that's my background
Who could ask for better? I am what I am.
I have no wish to be otherwise. But who I am,
That I must know. And I will know it!

OEDIPUS *remains on stage during the following chorus.*

CHORUS. If I can foretell the future,
Either by prophecy, or common sense,
I predict that by tomorrow morning
This truth will be dawning:
That mysterious Cithaeron,
That magical mountain
Was father and mother and nurse
To Oedipus our king,
And our voices will sing
Praises for his outlandish birth,
A child of the earth,
And glory to Apollo, and thanksgiving.

Or perhaps some skyborn Olympian
Brought him to birth, an immortal mother?

Maybe Pan, who goes roaming
The slopes at evening
Seduced a wild goddess
Of woodland or scree?
Or Apollo, who relishes high pasture,
Bred a son from a spirit?
Or Hermes, in his summit
Of Cyllene, did the deed?
Or was Dionysus' passionate seed
Sown on Helicon, where a nymph lay dreaming?

OEDIPUS. Elder statesmen of Thebes, I think I can see
The man we are waiting for: I'm making a guess,
I've never set eyes on him. But my men
Are bringing him, and he looks the same age
As this man from Corinth. Is he the one?
You should know him, you've seen him before.
CHORUS. I recognise him. This is the man.
He was Laius' servant, and honest as the day.
Enter the old SHEPHERD *escorted by palace servants or guards.*
OEDIPUS. Now, friend from Corinth, you speak first.
Is this the man you mean?
CORINTHIAN. It is.
OEDIPUS. And you, old shepherd. Look me in the eye,
And answer my questions. Did you work
For old King Laius?
SHEPHERD. Yes sir, I did.
I was born and bred in his service, not bought
In the market.
OEDIPUS. And what was your job here?
How were you employed?
SHEPHERD. For most of my life
I've been a shepherd, sir.
OEDIPUS. And where?
In what part of the country did you usually work?
SHEPHERD. Well . . . it would be . . . Cithaeron mostly,
All around there.
OEDIPUS. And this fellow here,
Have you ever seen him before?
SHEPHERD. What man
Do you mean, sir? How would I know him?

OEDIPUS. This man, standing here! Did you have any dealings
With him ever, that you remember?
SHEPHERD. I can't say . . .
Not just this minute. I can't remember . . .
CORINTHIAN. Of course, he's forgotten. But I'll soon remind him!
The days when us two were neighbours, up there
On Cithaeron, he won't forget that, will you?
He had two flocks, and I had one.
Three seasons altogether we were up there, the two of us,
From spring right through to autumn. Then I
Drove my lot down to Corinth, and he
Took his lot down to Thebes, to Laius' place.
Now, is that true, or isn't it?
SHEPHERD. Well. True enough. It's a long time ago.
CORINTHIAN. In that case, you won't have forgotten that boy,
The baby you gave me . . . You told me to look after it
And bring it up as my own.
SHEPHERD. Why
Are you asking about that? It's years ago.
CORINTHIAN. And he's a grown man! My dear old mate!
This is that baby!
SHEPHERD. God damn you, be quiet!
Keep your mouth shut!
OEDIPUS. Now now, old fellow,
You deserve that sharp tone more than he does.
SHEPHERD. Why, great king? What have I done wrong?
OEDIPUS. Not giving a straight answer
To a straight question. He asked you
About the child.
SHEPHERD. It's just talk. He knows nothing.
He doesn't understand.
OEDIPUS. Now listen.
If you won't speak willingly, you'll be forced to speak.
SHEPHERD. I'm an old man, sir. For god's sake don't hurt me.
OEDIPUS. You two, twist his arms back: quickly!
SHEPHERD. Oh, god help me now, what have I done
Sir, what more do you want to know?
OEDIPUS. This man is asking you about a child.
Was it you who gave him that child? Was it?
SHEPHERD. It was me. I wish I'd died that day!
OEDIPUS. You'll die today, unless you tell the truth.

SHEPHERD. I'll die if I tell it, as well, that's for sure.
OEDIPUS. This fellow is still determined to prevaricate.
SHEPHERD. No, no, I'm not. I told you, I gave it to him. What else?
OEDIPUS. Where did it come from? Was it your child?
Or did someone give it to you?
SHEPHERD. Not mine.
Would I give my own child away?
It came from someone else.
OEDIPUS. Who else?
From Thebes? From one of the citizens here?
What kind of house did that baby come from?
SHEPHERD. I beg you sir, by all the gods.
Don't ask me that!
OEDIPUS. I am asking.
If I must ask again, you're as good as dead!
SHEPHERD. Well . . . you see . . . it was born in Laius' house.
OEDIPUS. A slave? Or was it a blood relation?
SHEPHERD. I'm on the edge, sir. Must I say it?
OEDIPUS. Yes, we're both on the edge. I must hear you say it.
SHEPHERD. They did say the child was his.
But the queen, in the palace, she could tell you!
OEDIPUS. Do you mean she gave it to you?
SHEPHERD. Yes, sir.
She did.
OEDIPUS. Why? For what purpose?
SHEPHERD. To kill it, sir.
OEDIPUS. Her own child? Poor woman.
SHEPHERD. Yes, sir. There was some prophecy.
She was scared stiff.
OEDIPUS. What prophecy?
SHEPHERD. There was talk that the boy would kill his father.
OEDIPUS. And why, in the name of all the gods,
Did you give it to this man?
SHEPHERD. I couldn't
Kill it, master. I couldn't do it.
A little boy, only three days old.
I thought, 'He'll take it miles away
To his own country. It'll be all right.'
So he took it and saved its life. And now
It's all turned out like this. If you
Are that man, the boy my friend took to Corinth,

You were marked out for suffering, from the day you were born.
OEDIPUS. All. All of it. I know it all now.
Nothing left to find. It all came true,
Every single word. Let the night come.
Daylight has no mercy.
It shows too much, too clearly. Yes.
My conception, a crime.
My marriage a crime.
And that murder, committed on my own father.
I see it all now.
Exit OEDIPUS, *into the palace, as the attendants lead the old* SHEPHERD *and the* CORINTHIAN *away.*
CHORUS. Like a shadow thrown in the dust
Is the short life of man:
The sunlit generations
Pass into the night,
And happiness, like a bird in flight,
Flutters, and is gone.
We have seen Oedipus the king
Brought down to misery.
Suffering, brief happiness, pain,
Is mortal man's destiny.

Like a champion marksman, he shot down
The Sphinx in full flight.
The master of the gods' reward
Was kingship, and power
Over men, the prize of one hour
Of brilliant insight.
From that day he was king
In Thebes, like a solid wall
His power surrounded us, and we sang
Of the benefits of his rule.

Was there ever a reversal of fortune
More terrible than this?
How can any man endure
Such merciless agony?
Who was ever marked out by destiny
For suffering like his?
Oedipus, world-famous king,

When you sucked and fondled at the same breast
How could the flesh keep silent so long,
Where both son and father caressed?

Time is an all-seeing eye
That searches out hidden guilt
When it seems most secure,
Then brings down the knife
On the father and son who shared a wife.
And the blood that was spilt.
Son of our murdered king,
Why did you ever come here? Your destiny
Leaves me choking with tears: bringing
Salvation for us with your own misery.

Enter the MESSENGER, *running from the palace, terrified and desperate.*

MESSENGER. Senators! Counsellors. Wise men of the city!
If you have any feeling at all
For the royal family of Thebes, those descendants of Labdacus,
You can't hold back your tears, not when you hear
What I have to tell you, and see yourself
The terrible scene in the palace! In there
Things have been done, deliberate things
Of such horror, such self-mutilations,
That rivers could not wash away the blood,
And stain on the family will be everlasting!

CHORUS. Haven't we seen and suffered enough?
What more is there to say?

MESSENGER. First of all,
In the plainest language: the queen is dead.

CHORUS. Dead? How can she be dead? Poor woman!

MESSENGER. I'll tell you. She killed herself!
You haven't seen it, and count yourselves lucky!
I shall never be able to forget it. That image
Will always be with me now. I was there,
And I'll tell you what happened, as accurately as I can.
When she rushed into the palace, in anguish,
She went straight into the bedroom, tearing
Her hair out in handfuls, and muttering
Like a madwoman. She slammed the door,
And locked herself in: and we heard her shouting,

Something about Laius, her first husband,
Who's been dead for years, and the night
They conceived the son who was to kill him
And breed misbegotten children on his own mother.
Then it became confused. She screamed,
And beat upon the bed, where she had conceived
A husband by a husband, and children by a child.
I heard all that. Her actual death
Was behind the locked door: and Oedipus
Broke in at that point, raving up and down
The hall and howling for a sword,
So that all our eyes were fixed on him
And we all forgot what she was doing.
'That wife of mine, that wife and mother,'
He shouted, 'her fertile belly,
Twice it's been harvested, me and my children!'
Then he suddenly made for the door –
None of us told him – as though some premonition
Suddenly told him she was there. He bellowed
And shouted and shoulder-charged the doors,
And kicked them, till the bolts and hinges
Shattered, and he stumbled in . . .
We saw her, slowing turning in the air,
Swinging slightly, like a pendulum,
Strung up by the neck. She'd hanged herself.
The king ran to her, loosed the rope
And lifted her down, all the while groaning
Heartbreakingly, like an animal.
He laid her gently on the floor,
And then – this was unbearable, the worst
Of all – there were two golden brooches,
Pinned on her dress. He opened them up,
Held them high in the air, at arm's length,
And plunged them down into his eyeballs,
Screaming and groaning that his own guilt
And suffering were too great for his eyes to see it
That now they would both be in darkness for ever,
That he would never see again
Those he should never have seen, nor ever
Love those he should never have loved.
That's the way he went on, cursing himself

And stabbing his eyelids again and again,
Till his face was a mass of blood and tears,
Not drops of blood, but like a thunderstorm
Or cloudburst, gushing down his cheeks! . . .
So, they embraced in the crime and embraced
In the punishment too, man and wife together.
They were happy you know, for a long time.
The family was famous, and considered fortunate,
But from today, horror, pain and grief,
All the suffering men have a name for
Will make their names notorious, for ever.

CHORUS. Has he any relief? Or is the pain getting worse?

MESSENGER. He's yelling for someone to unbolt the doors
And drag him out, so that all Thebes will see
The father-killer and mother- . . .
I can't say that word in public. He's shouting
Repeatedly that he must be kicked out of the city.
He's exiled by his own decree, he mustn't
Stay long enough to bring down the curse
On his own family. But he's in pain,
And half his strength has gone, poor man.
He can't see, he needs someone to guide him,
And the physical agony must be much worse
Than any man can bear. You'll see yourself.
The doors are opening. Sorrow and pity
You must feel, when you see him with your own eyes.
His worst enemy couldn't wish him this.

Enter OEDIPUS, *blinded.*

CHORUS. Have any man's eyes ever seen
Sufferings more terrible? Mine have not.
What mania, what insanity has turned your brain,
Man of all sorrows? Some demon of the night,
Some destructive impulse in man, prowling
Silently round you, waiting its chance,
Has sprung with inhuman strength, howling
At your throat. I'm fascinated and repelled, in a trance
Of horror and pity. I want to watch your pain,
And to turn from it. I want to learn from your torments,
But I shudder at what that knowledge might mean.

OEDIPUS. Anguish, ah, agony . . .
Pity, someone. I can't see

Where my legs are taking me. Is that my voice,
Floating like a ghost in front of my face?
The punishment begins here. Where will the end be?
CHORUS. A place unspeakable to men's ears:
Horrors too dreadful for human eyes to see.

OEDIPUS. Dark now, all dark.
This nightmarish blackness surrounds me. I shall never
See daylight again. A black cloud, a thick fog, forever
Enfolds me like a cloak.
The pain in my eyes, ah gods, grinds sharper,
But the pain in my memory cuts deeper.
CHORUS. This is his life now: to suffer twice over:
The body's sharp pain, and the mind's dull ache.

OEDIPUS. My friends, are you there?
You don't desert me, still loyal, still kind:
You stay with me, although I am blind,
You give me your care.
I have no eyes now to see your face,
But I know you're here, by the sound of your voice.
CHORUS. Your mutilated eyes! What darkness in your mind,
What demon, could bring you to such despair?

OEDIPUS. Apollo, my friends, Apollo the god,
His power determined my agony!
But these eyes were blinded by my own hand.
Why have eyes to see
My own degradation and misery?
CHORUS. This is the truth: simple and hard.
OEDIPUS. Can the earth's loveliness, or all its beauty
Comfort eyes like mine? What music could I hear
To soothe such pain? What could I ever see
Or hope to see, to bring relief or cure?
Waste no more time. Take me from this city.
No one has ever been more damned. No pity
For the man all men curse and the gods abhor.
CHORUS. The pain in the flesh is doubled in the mind:
Ignorance made you happy. The truth has made you blind.

OEDIPUS. Damn the man who saw my ankles bleed

And cut me free from those straps! His mercy
Only made things worse. I should have died!
Did I live for this agony –
And for those that love me, a lifetime of misery?

CHORUS. Better a child's grave on the mountainside.

OEDIPUS. Now my name will be known for ever:
My father's killer, my mother's lover,
Husband and child, father and brother:
Born to cause suffering, and to suffer.
Will there be any horror or shame
Not synonymous with Oedipus' name,
Or ever a man more damned? No, never!

CHORUS. You bring blindness and exile on your own head
By this action. You would have been better dead.

OEDIPUS. No! You must never say that, never!
What has happened here, has happened for the best,
Don't dare tell me otherwise! If I could see,
How could I look my father in the face
When I meet him in the underworld?
Or my mother? No death could be punishment enough
For the horror of what I have done to her.
And my children, whom I love: what pleasure
For me to see their faces again
Conceived as they were conceived? My eyes
Are a father's eyes. What would they see?
And this marvellous city, in which I was born
The greatest among men: if I had eyes
I would still see its palaces and temples
Which by my own edict, my own folly,
My own insane determination, are forbidden
The murderer of Laius, the unclean thing
All men turn away from and the gods hate.
I mean myself. With eyes in my head,
How could I look anyone in the face,
Even the Theban people in the streets?
My hearing too, these ears! If I'd known a way
To block up these receivers, or cut them off
From every sound the world makes,
I'd have done that too, with no regrets.
To make a prison cell of my own mind

In solitary confinement from the world.
No sight or sound of all these horrors
Could touch me there. That would be peace . . .
The wastelands of Cithaeron, like a nurse,
Cradled me, kept me alive. For this.
Trees, gulleys, naked rocks,
You should have let me die. You preserved me
To parade before the world the well-kept secret
Of who my father was, and who my mother.
And Corinth, my childhood home,
And Polybus and Merope, whom I loved
And thought my parents, how could you imagine
What a corrupt man your open-faced boy
Would become in his age? If ever a rosebud
Was soggy and rotten within, if ever an apple
Was filthy with maggots, let these images
Describe me in my youth, born damned, among the damned.
And that triple junction under the trees,
That overgrown place where three roads meet,
Do the trees still remember, and the shady pathways,
What happened there, whose blood was spilt,
My father's, my own. On the way to Thebes
I was, that day, and what acts I did
When I got there, on the dead man's wife,
Entering so joyfully that same passage
That gave me exit into the world, sowing my seed
In the warm earth where I was germinated!
A marriage for a monster, father, brother,
Son, bride, wife, mother,
Children, sisters, all confused,
Horribly mingled in a liaison
Too filthy to give a name to, too corrupt
To be remembered with anything but loathing . . .
No more then, nothing, what should never
Have been done should never be spoken of . . .
Take me away quickly, for god's sake,
Hide me, as far from this city as a man
Can go, drown me, bury my body
Under the floor of the ocean!
The CHORUS *shrinks away from his groping hands.*
Where are you?

Is anyone there, or have you all gone?
For pity's sake, someone help me!
Don't leave me alone! Take me,
You need not draw back. It's not infectious,
This crime of mine! I'm the one
Who must bear the guilt and the punishment
And the shame. And I must bear it alone.

Enter CREON.

CHORUS. Creon is coming. It's up to him
Now, to deal with you. He will advise us,
And take action as provisional governor in your place.

OEDIPUS. Creon. Of course. There is nothing I can say
To him, and why should he listen to anything
I say? I treated him unjustly.

CREON. I haven't come to crow, Oedipus,
Now you are down, nor to accuse you
Of crimes, or misjudgements, committed in the past.

CREON *turns to* OEDIPUS' *attendants.*

But you people, if you have no respect
For the common decencies, the sympathy
Due to any man's sufferings, revere the sun
At least, whose warmth and brightness sustains us.
The open street, in broad daylight,
Is no place for a thing unclean,
Cursed and sentenced to be cast out.
Not even in the open air, on the common earth
Or under the rain from heaven, will he
Find welcome or shelter. Take him in. His sufferings
Are no business of the public. It's private,
A question of family grief and prayer,
A matter for his relations, not the whole city.

OEDIPUS. This is a kindness Creon, more
Than I expected in my degradation.
For your sake, not mine, let me ask one favour.

CREON. What favour? You need not go on your knees.

OEDIPUS. Get rid of me quickly. Deport me
To some empty wasteland, where the human voice
Is never heard.

CREON. I could have done that
Already, of course. But it seems wiser
As a matter of priority, to consult the oracle.

OEDIPUS. But the oracle has spoken, unambiguously!
Kill the father-killer. Cast out
The unclean thing. I am the man.
CREON. That's true, that's what was said. But in circumstances
As extraordinary as these, it seems safer
To consult the god again.
OEDIPUS. For what?
I am the cause of all this pain,
And the punishment is known. What is there to ask?
CREON. Haven't you, of all men, learned
To trust the gods?
OEDIPUS. Yes, I've learned that.
One favour more I must ask
Or beg. The woman who lies dead
In the palace, let her be buried
Decently, with whatever formalities
You think appropriate. She is your sister,
Your flesh and blood, and you owe her that.
In my case . . . Thebes is my country,
My homeland – though I never knew it
Until today – and my presence, alive,
Within her walls would be a curse
On her. Let me leave, and go up
Into my own mountains of Cithaeron.
My mother and father left me there
To die in the wilderness and I shall die now,
In accordance with their wishes who wished me dead.
My death, I know, will be mysterious.
My life was saved miraculously, and not
For the common death of old age or sickness,
But for some other ending – awe-inspiring
And full of terror. Let it come as it will.
But now . . . my children. The boys, Creon,
Polynices and Eteocles, they're almost men
And can look after themselves, wherever they go.
But the girls . . . they're so small, such babies yet.
They have shared everything with me, food and drink
And company. I doubt if they've ever so much
As eaten a meal away from their father.
Look after them Creon, for my sake . . .
And if I could . . . just once more,

Touch them, and share my tears
With theirs, just once, kindness
And generosity could do no more.
Grasping their hands and remembering,
I could imagine I had eyes
To see them once again, before I go.
The two young children, Antigone and Ismene, little girls of perhaps six and eight, have already been led in, and they stand before OEDIPUS.
Shh! I heard something! Are they here already?
Are they crying? You have taken pity
Creon, and brought them to me unasked.
The dearest of my children . . . Am I right?

CREON. I know how much you loved them, and love
Them still, in spite of everything.

OEDIPUS. God bless you Creon. May you have better luck
Both as a king and as a man, than I've had.
Children, where are you, come here to me.
Embrace me! Antigone, Ismene!
These are your brother's hands, and your father's,
The hands that blinded me. I was blind already
If the truth be known. I saw nothing
As I fathered you on my own mother,
Only a wife! Was ever a man more blind!
My eyes can't see you now, but they can
Cry still, and they do, when I think
What hard lives you will lead in the world
When you are grown up, the vicious things
People will say. Festivals,
And public holidays, no fun for you
They will be, staying at home in tears
While the others enjoy themselves. And later,
When you're old enough to be married, where
Is the man who will be brave, or foolhardy enough
To take you on, and that scandalous reputation
That will stick to all my children, and
My children's children. 'Their father killed
His father, then ploughed up that same ground
Where he sprouted, gave his own mother
Children, those girls, yes, they're his sisters!'
That's the sort of thing people will say.

And who will marry you in those circumstances?
Nobody will, my poor girls, virginity
And barrenness are all you can look forward to.
Creon, Menoeceus was your father,
And you must be their father now,
As nearest kin. The two of us
Who brought them into the world, we are both dead,
Or dead to them. They are quite alone,
Apart from you. Don't let them wander
As orphans through the world, homeless,
As well as husbandless, and don't condemn them
To share the punishment that falls on me.
They are very young, very poor now,
And if you don't help them, quite without hope.
Promise me, and take my hand upon the promise.
The two men grasp hands.
Good brother, good . . .
OEDIPUS *turns to the girls.*
If you were older
My girls, and could understand such things
I could tell you so much . . . but we'll leave that now.
When you say your prayers, ask for peace,
A place to call home, and a better life
Than your father has had.

CREON. That's enough. No more tears
In public. You must go inside.

OEDIPUS. No, not yet, just a moment longer –
Even against your better judgement.

CREON. No, everything must be done correctly,
The proper thing at the proper time!

OEDIPUS. On one condition! That I have your promise.

CREON. My promise?

OEDIPUS. To send me into exile.

CREON. That is the gods' decision not mine.
I shall follow their instructions.

OEDIPUS. Don't force me in there, when the gods hate me.

CREON. If they hate you, they will cast you out.

OEDIPUS. But do you agree? Will you do what I ask?

CREON. No. I shall do what I say I will do.

OEDIPUS. Well. I'm in your hands.

CREON. Then go in.

But leave the children here.

OEDIPUS. The children?

Don't take them away from me! Don't do that!

CREON. Don't give me orders! Those days are over.
Your orders have brought you to this.
Now you must learn to obey.

CREON *gestures to the Attendants, who take* OEDIPUS *into the palace.* CREON *follows them, leading the two children.*

CHORUS. People of Thebes, inheritors
Of the ancient city of our ancestors,
You have all seen Oedipus the king –
Who solved the riddle the she-monster sang
And by his genius saved the state,
And whose fame for that deed was so great
No man could but envy him –
Overwhelmed by a tidal wave
Of disasters that will sweep him to his grave.
Judge no man's life until he is dead.
There are no winners till the race is run.
Call no man fortunate, or safe from pain,
Till he lies in his last everlasting bed
And the earth covers his head.

Exit the CHORUS.

Notes

page

5 *Priest of Zeus*: Zeus was the king of the ancient Greek gods.
My children: a distinctive and unusual way of addressing the suppliants which highlights Oedipus' paternal and protective feelings towards his people as well as his authoritarian position.
King Cadmus: the founder of Thebes, father of Laius and grandfather of Oedipus.
laurel branches: it was a common custom for desperate people praying for divine intervention to carry branches of olive or laurel wreathed in wool and lay them on the altar of the god to whom supplication was being made.
prayers for the sick: these special prayers would be addressed to Apollo who was considered a healer of the sick.
Sitting: most probably kneeling in the position of supplication.
emblems like these: laurel branches and incense burners.
Pallas Athene: an unmarried goddess born from Zeus' forehead, deity of wisdom and patroness of handicrafts. Though female, she was portrayed dressed in armour and was often associated with martial virtue.
Ismenus' shrine: a shrine close to the Theban river, Ismenus. At shrines like this, the behaviour of burnt offerings was read by priests to foretell the future.

6 *This city is like a warship . . . blood*: a recurrent image in the play and a common metaphor in ancient Greek tragedy to describe the city-state.
some god: no specific god is held responsible for the city's plague.
the underworld: Hades, death.
It is not because we think of you as a god/But because we know you to be the best of men: an important remark which shows the proper view of a leader's status in democratic Greece.
riddle of the Sphinx: the Sphinx was a monstrous female creature associated with death and bad luck, depicted as a winged lion with a woman's head. According to the myth, as

recounted by the historian Apollodorus (born *c.* 130 BC), the Sphinx sat on Mount Phikion and asked the Thebans a riddle: 'What goes on four legs in the morning, two at noon and three in the evening?' Each time they gave the wrong answer she ate one of them. Oedipus gave the right answer which was 'man'.
magical tyranny: the term tyranny was ambiguous in ancient Greece and could mean either bad or good rule. In this case the word adopts a negative meaning. The adjective 'magical' highlights the supernatural nature of the Sphinx's hold, similar to a magic spell in fairy tales.
find us/Some remedy: the word 'remedy' implies Oedipus' role as curator and healer of the city.

7 *Creon, the son of Menoeceus*: Creon and Jocasta were the children of Menoeceus who was a descendant of the Sparti, the armed men who rose from the ground where the teeth of the dragon of Ares (god of war) had been sown by Cadmus. When an army from Argos laid siege to Thebes, the prophet Teiresias foretold that if one of the Sparti sacrificed himself to the god Ares, Thebes would be saved. Menoeceus therefore threw himself from the walls and the Thebans were indeed victorious.
oracle: the oracle, or mouthpiece of the gods, was consulted at certain sacred places, the most famous being the temple of Apollo at Delphi. The oracle's incomprehensible words were interpreted by the priests for ordinary mortals.
Apollo: the son of Zeus and Leto, he was considered to be the god of music and also of prophecy, colonisation, medicine, poetry and dance. In addition, he was also a god of light and known as Phoebus, and was sometimes identified with the sun god Helios. He was held to be the god of plague and according to Homer's *Iliad,* shot plague arrows into the Greek camp. Finally, as the god of healing and medicine, he had the power to purify those guilty of murder and other horrific crimes.
Pythia: the Pythia was the priestess at Apollo's oracle in Delphi and operated as a mouthpiece for the god. She sat on a bronze tripod in the inner chamber of the temple and received divine inspiration.

8 *Laius*: king of Thebes, son of Labdacus and father of Oedipus.

9 *house of gold*: the temple of Apollo at Delphi.

10 *island of Delos*: situated in a ring of islands called the Cyclades, in the Aegean Sea, Delos was the birthplace of Apollo and Artemis.

supreme physician: Apollo, god of medicine and healing.
Artemis: the daughter of Leto and Zeus, and the twin of Apollo. Artemis was the virgin goddess of the wilderness and hunting, as well as fertility.
days of disaster: at the time of the Sphinx's tyranny Thebes was also struck by plague, for which the Sphinx was held responsible, and which was thought to be a punishment for Laius' crime (see p. xv).
god of war: Ares.

11 *Thracian bay*: Thrace is a region in the north of Greece, commonly associated with Ares.
Amphitrite's bed: Amphitrite was the queen of the sea.
wolfish god-king: Zeus was sometimes called 'Zeus Lykaios' or 'Wolf-Zeus'. According to myth, while travelling through Arcadia, Zeus became very angry with Lycaon, king of Arcadia, and transformed him and his sons into wolves. A festival, known as the Festival of Lykaia, therefore took place on the slopes of Mount Lykaion in honour of Zeus. The rituals of the festival allegedly included a human sacrifice to Zeus. Whoever ate the human flesh would be turned into a wolf and could only return to human form by abstaining from eating human flesh for ten years.
Lycian slopes: Lycia is a region in Asia Minor.
Bacchus: also known as Dionysus, the son of Zeus by Semele. He was the god of wine and theatre. In contrast to the civilised Apollo, he was connected with darkness, nature and ecstatic behaviour through collective dancing.
Maenads: the female followers of the wine-god Dionysus and also called Bacchae. Inspired by him to ecstatic frenzy, they accompanied him and participated in his orgiastic rites.
this killing/God, whom the gods themselves despise: Ares, the god of war. Because of his cruel and warlike nature he was hated by all the gods and even his own father, Zeus, disliked him.

12 *wash in his house*: one of the collective rituals of a household included the washing of its members with holy water. Not to be allowed to participate in this ritual meant exclusion from the household.

13 *Agenor*: the Phoenician king of Tyros and a son of Poseidon. He was the father of Europa and Cadmus, founder of Thebes, great-grandfather of Laius, father of Oedipus.

justice be ours: the Greek word for justice was *dike*. *Dike* was the goddess of justice. Her mother, Themis, was the goddess of divine justice.

14 *Teiresias*: the famous blind seer who appears in many Greek tragedies escorted by a young boy. Teiresias also appears in Sophocles' *Antigone*.

15 *and many other omens*: as in *Antigone* when the prophet 'read' burnt offerings to the god.

17 *There was a monster here*: the Sphinx (see note to p. 6).

18 *scapegoat*: the idea that Oedipus has been turned into a scapegoat and is unfairly accused in order to cleanse the city from its pollution has been stressed in certain interpretations of the tragedy. For more, see commentary, pp. xxx–xxxii.

Cithaeron: a sacred mountain near Thebes where Oedipus was left to perish as an infant.

20 *rock of Delphi*: Delphi was the site of the sanctuary to Apollo, the legendary oracle Pythia and the Pythian Games. Its name may commemorate Apollo's cult, Delphinios, meaning dolphin. It is situated on Mount Parnassus. The rock is the chamber from which the oracle (Apollo's vessel) prophesied.

Thundering Zeus' son: Apollo, who is here portrayed exacting punishment with his father's lethal bolt of lightning and thunder (symbols of Zeus, father and leader of the gods who dwelt on Mount Olympus).

unsleeping Fates: agents of divine vengeance also known as Furies. They take a human form in the final part of Aeschylus' *Oresteia* trilogy, *Eumenides*.

Parnassus: Apollo's oracle and temple at Delphi lie on Mount Parnassus, in the region of Phocis. According to myth, Zeus had let loose two eagles who came together at Delphi, marking the centre of the Earth and also the point where Earth touched the divine.

21 *Polybus' son*: Oedipus. Polybus was the king of Corinth who, along with his wife Merope, raised Oedipus.

Labdacus: grandfather of Oedipus.

27 *How like a pilot . . . in rough weather or calm*: the ship and its captain was a common metaphor in Greek tragedy for the description of a king's relationship to his city.

its ankles were pierced . . . thongs: Oedipus (Swollen-foot) gets his name from the fact that he was left in the mountains with his ankles pinned together.

28 *Phocis*: a region divided in two by Mount Parnassus.
Daulia: the area north of the road from Thebes to Delphi.

29 *Merope*: adoptive mother of Oedipus and queen of Corinth.
Doris: a famous region of ancient Greece, close to Phocis.

32 *And justice, and belief in the moral law*: see note to p. 13 on justice. The moral law here refers to the sacred or 'unwritten laws'. They protected the relationship between kin, hosts and guests, and the living and the dead. In *Antigone*, the heroine passionately defends the laws of the gods – moral laws – against those made by men.
Olympus: Olympus is the highest mountain in Greece and for this reason its summit was considered to be the residence of the Olympian gods.

33 *tyrant*: here the term tyrant has a negative meaning and refers to an absolute ruler or dictator. The whole second stanza of this choral dance describes the alternatives for an all-powerful ruler: arrogance and disrespect will lead to downfall, while respect for the moral laws, the gods and the people will bring prosperity.
old wisdom and morality: see note to p. 32 on moral law.
Olympia: the sanctuary of Olympia, the most ancient and probably the most famous sanctuary in Greece, home of the Olympic Games. It is situated in the Alpheios valley in the western region of the Peloponnese.

34 *Like desperate sailors . . . despair*: a recurrent metaphor which reflects the dire situation in the city.
Corinth: a famous city in the northern Peloponnese, where Oedipus was raised by his adoptive parents, Polybus and Merope.

38 *Swollen foot*: see note to p. 27.

41 *Pan*: the god of shepherds and flocks, who was especially popular in the region of Arcadia. Also a god of fertility, with the legs of a goat, he chased nymphs through the forests and mountains. He was a son of the god Hermes.
Hermes: the son of Zeus and the nymph Maia, he was the god of shepherds, land travel, merchants, weights and measures, oratory, literature, athletics and thieves, and known for his cunning and shrewdness. Most importantly, he was the messenger of the gods.
Cyllene: a mountain in the region of Arcadia, the birthplace of Hermes.

Dionysus: see note to p. 11 on Bacchus.

Helicon: a mountain in the region of Boeotia, dedicated to the Muses.

not bought/In the market: if slaves were not bought in the market but brought up in the household of their owner they were considered more loyal to their masters and were usually treated much better, almost as part of the family.

42 *Three seasons altogether we were up there . . . autumn*: a pattern followed by Greek shepherds even today: for the summer months they move their flocks from lowlands to the high mountains.

you'll be forced to speak: Oedipus' impatience and violent temper start to get out of control.

45 *all-seeing eye*: from now on the issues of blindness and sight, darkness and light, become central and are reflected through a number of descriptions and ironic statements. Oedipus who is about to blind himself physically is also about to see the truth.

52 *Polynices and Eteocles . . . Antigone and Ismene*: Oedipus' sons have killed one another at the beginning of Sophocles' *Antigone*, triggering a moral dilemma for Antigone and Ismene which leads to further tragedy. The fight between the brothers is dealt with by Aeschylus in *Seven Against Thebes*.

Questions for Further Study

1. How far do you think that the ancient Greek spectators' familiarity with the story of Oedipus affected their perception of the play?
2. In what ways are Athenian culture, religion and politics reflected in Sophocles' version of *Oedipus the King*?
3. Many of the events of the Oedipus myth, such as the killing of his father, solving the riddle of the Sphinx, have already taken place when the tragedy opens. Why does Sophocles choose to concentrate on this moment in Oedipus' life?
4. Aristotle's ideal plot structure was that of *Oedipus the King*. Do you agree with him and for what reasons?
5. Consider how the ritual and festival context (dances, prayers, sacrifices) of the ancient theatrical performance could have affected (a) the staging of *Oedipus the King*; and (b) the audience's perception of *Oedipus the King*. How would this affect your own staging of the tragedy?
6. Do you think that the formal ancient theatrical conventions (space, masks, poetic language, chorus, etc.) could still work on an emotional level for a modern audience of *Oedipus the King*?
7. Consider whether rhetoric ('the art of persuasion' in speech-making) could have informed or influenced the acting of *Oedipus the King*?
8. To what extent could the chorus be seen as a jury?
9. How could rhetoric co-exist with masked acting (loss of identity under the mask/persona of the mythic character)? Using *Oedipus the King* as an example, in its political and ritual aspects, consider the paradox of acting in ancient Greek theatre (getting lost in the mask/being conscious of performing).
10. Part of Sophocles' skill as a dramatist was the inclusion of dialogue between three characters that was used in successively more complex scenes, generating triangular patterns of speech. Consider the significance of the third actor in *Oedipus the King* as well as the advantages it brings in the emotional development of the play.

DON TAYLOR was a playwright and poet, and a director of plays in all the media, as well as a translator of Greek drama. In the early 1980s he translated Sophocles' Theban plays: *Oedipus the King*, *Oedipus at Colonus* and *Antigone*. He directed the trilogy for BBC TV and it was broadcast on consecutive nights in 1986. He went on to translate three of Euripides' war plays: *Iphigenia at Aulis*, *The Women of Troy* and *Helen*, the first of which was televised in 1989. His own stage plays include *The Rose of Evam*, *The Exorcism*, *Brotherhood*, *Daughters of Venice*, *Retreat from Moscow*, *When the Barbarians Came* and *The Road to the Sea*. Including works for radio and television, he wrote more than fifty plays and films, among them three verse plays. He died in 2003.

ANGIE VARAKIS received her first degree in Theatre Studies from the University of Patras in Greece and her MA and PhD in Drama and Theatre from Royal Holloway, University of London. Her research interests involve the performance practice of Greek theatre with a special emphasis on the use of masks in modern productions of Greek drama. She has participated in a series of international conferences on the modern staging of ancient drama and contributed to the electronic journal *Didaskalia* and to the forthcoming *Blackwell's Companion to Classical Receptions*, ed. Lorna Hardwick and Chris Stray, and *Aristophanes in Performance, 421 BC–2005 AD: Peace, Birds, Frogs*, ed. Edith Hall and Amanda Wrigley, published by Legenda. She is a lecturer in Drama at the University of Kent at Canterbury.